EMOTIONAL CONDITIONING

A GUIDE TO WATSONIAN PSYCHOLOGY

TABLE OF CONTENTS

INTRODUCTION TO EMOTIONAL CONDITIONING

Preliminary Considerations

Emotional conditioning, a crucial concept in the field of psychology, denotes the process through which an individual's emotional responses are shaped and altered by their experiences. Originating from the seminal work of behaviorist psychologists, most notably John B. Watson and B.F. Skinner, emotional conditioning has become a fundamental aspect of understanding human behavior and mental processes. The evolution of this concept can be traced back to Watson's famous Little Albert experiment, where he demonstrated the potential for emotional responses to be elicited and modified through classical conditioning. This groundbreaking study laid the groundwork for the subsequent exploration of emotional conditioning and its implications for psychological research and practice.

The significance of emotional conditioning in psychological research and practice cannot be overstated. It elucidates the mechanisms underlying the acquisition and modification of emotional responses, shedding light on the interplay between external stimuli and internal affective states. As such, it has been instrumental in informing therapeutic interventions aimed at addressing maladaptive emotional reactions and disorders. Furthermore, the study of emotional conditioning has contributed to the advancement of various psychological theories, including behaviorism, cognitive psychology, and psychopathology.

Key figures in the development of emotional conditioning, such as Ivan Pavlov, John B. Watson, and B.F. Skinner, have significantly shaped our current understanding of emotional learning and behavioral adaptation. Their pioneering contributions have laid the groundwork for empirical investigations into the nature of emotional conditioning, fostering a rich and diverse body of knowledge within the discipline of psychology. By delving into the historical context and foundational studies that have delineated the contours of emotional conditioning, researchers and practitioners gain valuable insights into the theoretical underpinnings and practical applications of this concept.

Significance in Psychological Research and Practice

Emotional conditioning represents a fundamental building block in the understanding and treatment of emotional disorders. Its influence has permeated diverse fields such as behavioral psychology, cognitive neuroscience, and psychotherapy, shaping the landscape of modern mental health interventions. By dissecting the mechanisms through which emotions become associated with specific stimuli or contexts, emotional conditioning unlocks invaluable insights into the origins and manifestations of anxiety, phobias, and other maladaptive emotional responses.

Psychological research has continuously underscored the pivotal role of emotional conditioning in elucidating the etiology of various psychopathologies. Through meticulously designed experiments and longitudinal studies, researchers have elucidated how past experiences can embed lasting emotional imprints, thereby influencing an individual's future behavioral and physiological reactions. Moreover, the versatility of emotional conditioning paradigms allows for the investigation of diverse clinical phenomena, ranging from the development of substance use disorders to the maintenance of chronic pain conditions. This multifaceted utility cements its status as a cornerstone in unraveling the complexities of human emotional experience.

The practical implications of emotional conditioning extend far beyond the confines of laboratory settings, permeating the domains of psychological assessment and therapeutic intervention. Clinicians adept in the nuances of emotional conditioning wield a potent tool for deciphering the tapestries of their clients' emotional struggles, enabling targeted interventions that foster healing and resilience. Whether through exposure-based therapies for trauma survivors or systematic desensitization techniques for individuals grappling with irrational fears, the integration of emotional conditioning principles empowers mental health professionals to address the root causes of emotional distress with precision and efficacy.

In essence, the significance of emotional conditioning in psychological research and practice lies in its unique ability to illuminate the interplay between environmental cues, affective experiences, and adaptive or maladaptive responses. A profound comprehension of these interwoven dynamics not only pioneers groundbreaking advancements in our theoretical understanding of human behavior but also serves as a catalyst for transformative healing in the lives of those grappling with the labyrinth of emotional afflictions.

Definitions and Core Concepts

Emotional conditioning, as a psychological process, is primarily concerned with the formation and modification of emotional responses through associative learning. At its core, emotional conditioning involves the acquisition of specific emotional reactions to neutral stimuli that are paired with emotionally significant events, resulting in the development of conditioned emotional responses. Central to this concept is the understanding that emotions are not solely innate but can also be shaped by environmental and experiential factors.

Key to grasping emotional conditioning is the distinction between unconditioned and conditioned stimuli and responses. Unconditioned stimuli (UCS) naturally elicit an emotional reaction without prior learning, such as fear in response to loud noises. Unconditioned responses (UCR) are the natural emotional reactions evoked by these stimuli. Conversely, conditioned stimuli (CS) are initially neutral but become associated with the UCS during the conditioning process. Conditioned responses (CR) are the learned emotional reactions generated by the CS after conditioning. This dichotomy forms the basis for understanding how emotional conditioning operates and how it can be applied to various situations.

The temporal relationship between stimuli and responses plays a crucial role in emotional conditioning. Delayed conditioning involves presenting the CS before the UCS, while simultaneous conditioning presents both stimuli at the same time. Trace conditioning introduces a temporal gap between CS offset and UCS onset. Each form of conditioning contributes to our understanding of how emotions are linked to specific cues and events in the environment.

Central to the concept of emotional conditioning is also the process of extinction, wherein the previously established association between CS and UCS weakens or diminishes over time due to the absence of reinforcement. Understanding the nuances of extinction processes is essential for addressing maladaptive emotional responses and developing effective therapeutic interventions.

Emotional conditioning is closely tied to concepts of emotional generalization and discrimination. Generalization occurs when similar stimuli evoke the same conditioned response, while discrimination involves the ability to differentiate between stimuli and generate specific responses accordingly. These phenomena shed light on the complexity of emotional conditioning and provide insights into how emotions can be modulated or refined through selective learning experiences.

Basic Principles of Emotional Learning

Emotional learning, a fundamental component of emotional conditioning, encompasses the cognitive and affective processes through which individuals acquire, process, and express emotional responses to stimuli. This phenomenon operates within the broader framework of behaviorism and cognitive psychology, illuminating the mechanisms underlying emotional development and reactivity. At its core, emotional learning is guided by several foundational principles that shape an individual's emotional repertoire and adaptive behavior.

One key principle of emotional learning is classical conditioning, as first expounded by Ivan Pavlov and subsequently integrated into the understanding of emotional responses. Through repeated associations between a neutral stimulus and an emotionally salient event, individuals develop conditioned emotional responses, such as fear, joy, or aversion. This process elucidates the role of environmental cues in shaping emotional reactions and lays the groundwork for understanding how emotions become ingrained through experience.

The concept of operant conditioning, as advanced by B.F. Skinner, plays a pivotal role in emotional learning. By emphasizing the consequences of behavior, operant conditioning elucidates how emotional expressions are shaped and reinforced by their outcomes. Positive reinforcement, negative reinforcement, and punishment all contribute to the modulation and acquisition of emotional responses, thereby underscoring the interplay between environmental contingencies and emotional learning processes.

Emotional learning also encompasses the notion of emotional contagion, wherein individuals reciprocally transmit and mimic the emotional states of others. This social phenomenon not only facilitates the dissemination of emotional experiences within interpersonal contexts but also underscores the significance of empathic processes and social learning in emotional development.

The neurobiological underpinnings of emotional learning are increasingly elucidated, with advances in neuroscience shedding light on the interplay between neural circuits, neurotransmitters, and emotional memory consolidation. The amygdala, prefrontal cortex, and hippocampus are among the key brain regions implicated in emotional learning, orchestrating the encoding, retrieval, and modulation of emotionally charged stimuli.

Theoretical Underpinnings and Philosophical Assumptions

At its core, emotional conditioning draws from behaviorist principles proposed by Ivan Pavlov and John B. Watson. These foundational theories emphasize the significance of observable behaviors and environmental stimuli in shaping emotional responses and learning processes. Moreover, the philosophical assumptions underlying emotional conditioning are deeply intertwined with the nature versus nurture debate, which explores the relative contributions of genetics and environmental factors in human development.

One key theoretical underpinning of emotional conditioning lies in the principle of stimulus-response associations. According to this perspective, emotional responses are learned through the repeated pairing of a neutral stimulus with a biologically significant event or another pre-existing emotional response. This process leads to the formation of strong associative links between the previously neutral stimulus and the emotional reaction, ultimately resulting in the elicitation of the emotional response through the presentation of the stimulus alone. As such, emotional conditioning theory heavily relies on the concept of associative learning, where the acquisition and modification of emotional responses are governed by the relationships between stimuli and behavioral outcomes.

The theoretical underpinnings of emotional conditioning also encompass cognitive components, particularly the role of cognition in mediating emotional responses. While traditional behaviorist theories primarily focus on observable behaviors and environmental contingencies, modern perspectives within emotional conditioning have integrated cognitive elements to account for the complex cognitive processes involved in emotional learning. These cognitive underpinnings highlight the influence of attention, memory, and perception in shaping emotional responses, thereby extending the theoretical framework of emotional conditioning beyond purely behaviorist paradigms.

Philosophically, emotional conditioning raises profound questions regarding the determinants of human emotions and the plasticity of emotional experiences. This domain of inquiry intersects with broader philosophical debates concerning free will, determinism, and the malleability of human nature. By exploring the philosophical assumptions underpinning emotional conditioning, researchers and practitioners can gain deeper insights into the implications of this theory for understanding human behavior, emotional regulation, and psychological interventions.

Comparison with Related Psychological Constructs

In delving into the sphere of emotional conditioning, it is essential to explore its intersection with other psychological constructs and theories. One such comparison lies in contrasting emotional conditioning with classical and operant conditioning, both of which are foundational concepts in behaviorism. While emotional conditioning shares commonalities with these forms of learning, it also distinguishes itself through the nature of the conditioned response, which often involves affective or emotional reactions rather than simply observable behaviors.

The role of cognition and mental processes in emotional conditioning invites a comparison with cognitive theories of emotion, notably the appraisal theory and the facial feedback hypothesis. Understanding how cognitive evaluations and interpretations influence emotional responses provides valuable insights into the complexity of emotional conditioning, highlighting the interplay between cognitive and behavioral components.

The broader spectrum of emotions and their regulation prompts a juxtaposition with emotion regulation theories, particularly those focusing on strategies for modifying emotional experiences and expressions. By examining emotional conditioning alongside these regulatory frameworks, researchers can gain a comprehensive understanding of how emotional responses are shaped, reinforced, and modulated within individuals and across diverse contexts.

Another area of overlap emerges when considering the developmental aspects of emotional conditioning in relation to developmental psychology, attachment theory, and social learning theory. Recognizing the ways in which early experiences, attachment styles, and social influences contribute to the formation of emotional responses underscores the interconnectedness of emotional conditioning with developmental processes and social interactions.

Additionally, the consideration of individual differences and personality traits in emotional conditioning aligns with personality theories, such as trait theory and psychodynamic perspectives that emphasize the role of unconscious dynamics in shaping emotional experiences. By integrating these perspectives, a more nuanced comprehension of how individual variations in emotional reactivity and regulation intersect with the processes of emotional conditioning can be achieved.

Common Misconceptions and Clarifications

Misconceptions surrounding emotional conditioning have persisted due to misinformation, oversimplification, and conflating it with other psychological processes. One prevalent misconception is the belief that emotional conditioning only involves the acquisition of fear responses, ignoring the expansive range of emotions that can be conditioned. This oversimplification detracts from the nuanced nature of emotional conditioning, which encompasses both positive and negative emotions, as well as complex emotional associations.

Another common misconception pertains to the permanence of conditioned emotional responses. While initial conditioning may appear enduring, subsequent research suggests that these associations can be modified and even extinguished through various techniques such as systematic desensitization and counterconditioning. Understanding the plasticity of emotional conditioning is crucial for dispelling the misconception that once an emotional response is conditioned, it is fixed and unchangeable.

Misguided beliefs often arise regarding the role of cognition in emotional conditioning. Contrary to the misconception that conditioning bypasses cognitive processes, contemporary theories acknowledge the interplay between cognitive appraisal and emotional learning. This acknowledgment highlights the need to clarify that emotional conditioning is not solely a product of automatic, reflexive reactions but is influenced by cognitive evaluations and interpretations.

One pertinent clarification involves addressing the misunderstanding of the ethical implications of studying emotional conditioning, particularly in relation to human subjects. Ethical considerations and guidelines govern the use of conditioning techniques in research and emphasize the utmost importance of informed consent, debriefing, and minimizing distress. By elucidating these ethical standards, it becomes evident that the responsible study of emotional conditioning prioritizes participant welfare and autonomy.

There is a widespread misconception surrounding the applicability of emotional conditioning exclusively to individuals, neglecting its relevance in societal and cultural contexts. Emotional conditioning extends beyond individual experiences and permeates societal norms, cultural rituals, and group identities. Recognizing this broad scope necessitates dispelling the misconception that emotional conditioning is confined to individual circumstances.

Methodological Approaches

Researching emotional conditioning involves a meticulous approach to designing and executing studies that capture the intricacies of human behavior and emotional responses. Methodological approaches in studying emotional conditioning encompass various techniques and tools aimed at understanding the mechanisms of how emotions are learned, unlearned, and influenced by external stimuli. Researchers employ a range of methods to investigate emotional conditioning, each with its unique strengths and limitations. Experimental studies form a cornerstone of methodological approaches, often utilizing classical and operant conditioning paradigms to investigate emotional responses. Through controlled stimulus presentations and behavioral measurements, researchers can map the acquisition, extinction, and generalization of emotional responses, shedding light on the underlying cognitive and physiological processes. Furthermore, physiological measures such as electrodermal activity, heart rate variability, and neuroimaging techniques like functional magnetic resonance imaging (fMRI) and electroencephalography (EEG) provide invaluable insights into the neural substrates and autonomic correlates of emotional conditioning. These approaches enable researchers to decode the interplay between cognition, emotion, and physiological arousal, offering a comprehensive understanding of emotional learning. Ethical considerations play a pivotal role in the methodological framework of emotional conditioning research. As emotional conditioning studies often involve exposure to emotional stimuli, ensuring participant welfare and informed consent is paramount. Ethical guidelines govern the treatment of human and animal subjects to protect their rights and minimize harm. Additionally, longitudinal and cross-sectional designs contribute to the methodological repertoire, enabling researchers to examine the development and persistence of conditioned emotional responses over time and across diverse populations. Moreover, advances in technology have brought forth innovative methodologies, including virtual reality simulations and ambulatory assessments, allowing for ecologically valid investigations of emotional conditioning within real-world contexts. These cutting-edge approaches afford researchers the opportunity to explore the dynamic nature of emotional conditioning in everyday environments, providing a holistic view of emotional responsiveness. Integrating diverse methodological approaches fosters a multidimensional understanding of emotional conditioning, enriching the field with nuanced insights and potential applications in clinical, educational, and organizational settings.

Relevance to Contemporary Psychological Issues

As the world grapples with an array of mental health concerns and behavioral challenges, understanding how emotional conditioning influences human thought, emotion, and behavior is essential. In today's society, it is evident that individuals are continuously bombarded with a myriad of stimuli that can shape their emotional responses and subsequent actions. From the pervasive influence of social media to the impact of traumatic events on a global scale, the role of emotional conditioning in shaping psychological well-being is undeniable.

One of the key contemporary psychological issues that intersects with emotional conditioning is the prevalence of anxiety disorders and phobias. Emotional conditioning offers valuable insights into the development and perpetuation of these conditions, as individuals can develop irrational fears and heightened anxiety responses through associative learning. By examining the process of fear acquisition and its maintenance through emotional conditioning, psychologists and therapists can devise targeted interventions to alleviate and manage these debilitating conditions.

The rise of technology and virtual environments has brought about new dimensions to the study of emotional conditioning. The immersive nature of virtual reality allows researchers to simulate and manipulate emotional triggers, providing a unique platform to understand the intricacies of emotional responses in controlled settings. This advancement not only enhances our comprehension of emotional conditioning but also paves the way for innovative therapeutic applications in treating various psychological disorders.

Another pressing contemporary issue that underscores the significance of emotional conditioning is the prevalence of addiction, including substance abuse and problematic behaviors. Emotional conditioning elucidates the role of associative learning in the reward pathways of the brain, shedding light on the mechanisms through which individuals develop and sustain addictive behaviors. Recognizing the impact of environmental cues and conditioned emotional responses in addiction opens avenues for developing comprehensive treatment strategies that address both the cognitive and emotional components of addictive behaviors.

The growing emphasis on cultural diversity and its implications for mental health brings forth the need to examine emotional conditioning within diverse societal contexts. Understanding how cultural norms, values, and experiences influence emotional responses and conditioning processes is crucial in providing culturally sensitive and effective psychological interventions. By acknowledging the interplay between cultural factors and emotional conditioning, psychologists can tailor therapeutic approaches that resonate with the lived experiences and sociocultural backgrounds of diverse populations, thereby promoting inclusivity and equity in mental health care.

Overall, the integration of emotional conditioning research with contemporary psychological issues holds immense promise in advancing our understanding of human behavior and enhancing the efficacy of psychological interventions. By addressing these cutting-edge intersections, this book aims to contribute to the ongoing dialogue surrounding the relevance of emotional conditioning in tackling the multifaceted challenges of modern-day psychology.

HISTORICAL CONTEXT AND DEVELOPMENT

Early Theories of Emotion in Psychological Science

Early psychology witnessed the emergence of various theories and conceptualizations regarding emotion, reflecting the intellectual milieu of the time. The early attempts to define and understand emotion were deeply rooted in philosophical and introspective traditions, with notable figures such as William James and Carl Lange proposing influential theories. James-Lange theory, for instance, posited that emotional experience arises from the perception of bodily changes, an idea that challenged traditional views of emotion as solely arising from conscious experiences. Similarly, the emergence of functionalism as a psychological approach emphasized the adaptive functions of emotions within organisms and the role of environmental influences on shaping emotional responses. Concurrently, Sigmund Freud's psychoanalytic theory highlighted the unconscious determinants of emotion, shedding light on the interplay between conscious and unconscious processes in emotional experiences. These early theories set the stage for later developments in understanding the complexities of emotion within the sphere of psychological science. Moreover, the evolution of these theories underscored the foundational shifts occurring within the discipline, laying the groundwork for the eventual rise of behaviorism as a dominant paradigm in psychology. As psychology transitioned towards a more empirical and experimental approach, marked by the pivotal work of Ivan Pavlov and the subsequent development of classical conditioning, the conceptualization of emotion underwent a significant transformation. The shift towards a behaviorist-oriented framework prioritized observable behaviors and external stimuli as key determinants of emotional reactions, ushering in a new era of experimental inquiry into the nature of emotions. This shift not only revolutionized the theoretical underpinnings of emotional studies but also paved the way for a more rigorous and systematic investigation of emotional processes.

Beginnings of Conditioning - Pavlov's Groundwork

Pavlov's groundbreaking work in classical conditioning laid the foundation for our understanding of how learned associations can shape emotional and behavioral responses. Ivan Petrovich Pavlov, a Russian physiologist, conducted his seminal research on the digestive system and inadvertently discovered the principles of classical conditioning. He observed that dogs salivated in response to the sight or smell of food, a natural reflexive action. However, through a series of carefully designed experiments, he demonstrated that the dogs began to salivate at the sound of a bell, when the two stimuli were repeatedly paired together. This led to the theory of conditioned reflexes, where an initially neutral stimulus (the bell) became associated with the unconditioned stimulus (the food) and elicited a conditional response (salivation). The profound implications of Pavlov's work extended beyond the field of physiology and into the field of psychology. His findings highlighted the role of environmental stimuli in shaping behavior and emotions, challenging the prevailing notion of instinctual determinism. These discoveries paved the way for the development of behaviorism and the study of emotional conditioning. Moreover, Pavlov's research laid the groundwork for subsequent explorations in associative learning, providing a framework for understanding how environmental cues can trigger emotional responses. The concept of conditioned responses, as elucidated by Pavlov, played a pivotal role in shaping modern theories of emotion and psychological interventions. Pavlov's work not only revolutionized our comprehension of the mind-body connection but also profoundly influenced the trajectory of psychological inquiry. Through his meticulous observations and systematic experimentation, Pavlov established the fundamental principles of conditioning that continue to inform contemporary research in emotional psychology and therapeutic practices.

Emergence of Behaviorism - Foundations and Principles

The foundations of behaviorism can be traced to the pioneering work of psychologists such as John B. Watson, who sought to establish a scientific approach to understanding and predicting behavior by focusing solely on observable and measurable phenomena. One of the key principles underpinning behaviorism is the rejection of introspection and unobservable mental processes as legitimate subjects for scientific inquiry. Instead, behaviorists emphasized the importance of studying external behaviors that could be objectively observed and quantified in experimental settings. This shift towards a more objective and empirical methodology laid the groundwork for a systematic and rigorous approach to psychological research. Central to the principles of behaviorism is the concept of operant conditioning, elucidated by B.F. Skinner. This influential theory posits that behavior is shaped and modified by its consequences, with reinforcement and punishment playing pivotal roles in the learning process. The emphasis on environmental stimuli and responses as determinants of behavior distinguishes behaviorism from earlier psychological perspectives and has had lasting implications for both research and applied domains within the discipline. Furthermore, behaviorism also emphasizes the significance of the environment in shaping individual behavior and rejects the notion of innate tendencies or traits governing behavior. This focus on environmental determinants has been instrumental in informing therapeutic interventions and behavior modification techniques aimed at fostering adaptive behaviors and ameliorating maladaptive ones. In addition, behaviorism advocates for the use of experimental methods, particularly controlled laboratory experiments, as a means of rigorously testing hypotheses and deriving general principles about behavior. This empirical orientation has been invaluable in advancing our understanding of various aspects of human behavior and has established behaviorism as a cornerstone of modern psychology. The influence of behaviorism extends beyond the confines of academic psychology, permeating fields such as education, clinical psychology, and organizational behavior, where its principles have been harnessed to develop effective interventions and strategies.

John B. Watson's Early Contributions

John B. Watson, revolutionized the study of human behavior by emphasizing the objective and observable aspects of psychological phenomena. His seminal work laid the groundwork for the systematic examination of emotional responses and their conditioning. Watson's break from introspective methods and focus on experimental research marked a significant shift in the field of psychology. Central to his approach was the belief that all behavior, including emotional reactions, could be understood through the principles of conditioning. Watson's early exploration into the conditioning of emotions influenced subsequent research and therapeutic practices. One of his pioneering demonstrations of emotional conditioning, the case of Little Albert, remains a controversial hallmark of behavioral psychology. The ethical implications and methodological details of this study continue to provoke debate and scrutiny among contemporary scholars. Watson's commitment to rigorous empirical investigation and his influential theoretical framework have left an indelible mark on the study of emotional conditioning. His emphasis on environmental determinants of behavior continues to shape modern perspectives on the nature and development of emotions. Furthermore, Watson's conceptualization of emotional conditioning has permeated various practical domains, including education, advertising, and clinical intervention.

The Little Albert Experiment - Methodology and Findings

The Little Albert experiment, conducted by John B. Watson and his graduate student Rosalie Rayner in 1920, is a pivotal study in the sphere of emotional conditioning. The methodology employed in this groundbreaking experiment was both innovative and controversial for its time, yielding profound insights into the acquisition and generalization of fear responses in young children. The primary objective of the study was to investigate whether specific emotional reactions, such as fear, could be induced through classical conditioning in an infant.

The researchers selected a healthy 9-month-old infant, referred to as Albert B., to serve as the subject of their study. Albert was initially unafraid of various stimuli, including rats and other furry objects. The experiment proceeded by introducing a white laboratory rat to Albert in conjunction with a loud, jarring noise produced by striking a metal rod with a hammer behind the child's back. This association between the presence of the rat and the startling noise aimed to condition a fear response in Albert towards the previously neutral stimulus, namely the rat.

Through systematic exposure to the rat-noise pairing over several sessions, Albert began to exhibit signs of distress and avoidance when presented with the rat alone, even in the absence of the accompanying loud noise. This pivotal finding highlighted the successful induction of a fear response through conditioned associations, thereby demonstrating the malleability of emotional responses through environmental stimuli.

The study extended its investigation beyond the initial observation of fear towards rats, revealing that Albert's conditioned fear had generalized to other similar stimuli, such as rabbits, dogs, and fur coats. This broadening of fear responses across comparable objects underscored the concept of stimulus generalization, further solidifying the foundational principles of emotional conditioning proposed by Watson and Rayner.

Despite the invaluable contributions of the Little Albert experiment to our understanding of behavioral psychology, the ethical considerations surrounding the treatment of the infant subject have sparked debates within the scientific community. The use of a vulnerable child in such a distressing experimental setup raises complex questions about the ethical boundaries of psychological research and the protection of human subjects.

Nevertheless, the impact of the Little Albert experiment on the field of psychology cannot be understated, as it continues to stimulate ongoing discussions on the ethical responsibilities of researchers and the potential implications of early childhood experiences on emotional development and psychopathology.

Interwar Period Discoveries and Theoretical Advancements

The interwar period marked a significant phase in the evolution of emotional conditioning as a formal scientific concept. During this time, there was an increased focus on the systematic study of human behavior, leading to several critical discoveries and theoretical advancements that shaped the trajectory of emotional conditioning research. Scholars and psychologists delved into exploring the complexities of conditioned emotional responses and sought to expand the foundational principles established by earlier pioneers such as John B. Watson and Ivan Pavlov.

One of the key developments during this era was the refinement of experimental methodologies for studying emotional conditioning. Researchers began to emphasize the importance of rigorous experimental design and standardized protocols to ensure the validity and reliability of their findings. This shift towards methodological precision paved the way for more nuanced investigations into the intricacies of emotional responses and the factors that influence their acquisition and expression.

Simultaneously, interwar psychological discourse witnessed a surge in interdisciplinary collaborations, with insights from physiology, neurology, and other scientific disciplines being integrated into the study of emotional conditioning. This multidisciplinary approach facilitated a more holistic understanding of the underlying mechanisms involved in the formation and modulation of conditioned emotional responses. It also contributed to the development of comprehensive theoretical frameworks that sought to elucidate the complex interplay between environmental stimuli, cognitive processes, and emotional reactions.

The interwar period saw the emergence of influential theoretical models that aimed to provide in-depth explanations of emotional conditioning phenomena. Notable scholars proposed conceptual frameworks that underscored the role of cognitive factors, attentional processes, and associative learning mechanisms in shaping emotional responses. These theoretical advancements not only enriched the theoretical landscape of emotional conditioning but also laid the groundwork for further empirical investigations and theoretical refinements in subsequent decades.

Post-war Era and the Expansion of Behaviorist Thought

In the post-war era, behaviorist thought experienced a significant expansion as advancements in technology and methodologies allowed for more detailed investigations into emotional conditioning. Notably, the development of new research tools such as operant conditioning chambers, or 'Skinner boxes,' provided researchers with greater control over experimental conditions, enabling them to explore the nuances of emotional responses with unprecedented precision.

This period saw an intensification of interest in emotional conditioning across various disciplines, leading to a surge in interdisciplinary collaborations. Psychologists, neuroscientists, and even ethologists joined forces to delve deeper into the underlying mechanisms of emotional conditioning, drawing from diverse perspectives to enrich the understanding of this complex phenomenon.

The post-war period also witnessed the burgeoning influence of behaviorism beyond the confines of academic research, permeating into applied fields such as clinical psychology and education. Behaviorist principles were increasingly incorporated into therapeutic interventions, paving the way for behavior modification techniques that proved instrumental in addressing a wide array of emotional and behavioral challenges.

The global sociopolitical landscape of the post-war years spurred an intensified focus on emotional resilience and adaptation. The atrocities of war had generated a pressing need to understand and address the psychological scars endured by individuals and communities, prompting behaviorists to explore the malleability of emotional responses and the potential for their reconfiguration through systematic conditioning.

Amidst this expansion, debates and discussions emerged within the behaviorist community, fostering a rich tapestry of theories, methodologies, and applications. This intellectual ferment propelled rapid advancements in the field of emotional conditioning, as scholars engaged in rigorous discourse and empirical scrutiny to refine their conceptualizations and practices.

However, alongside this period of growth, behaviorist thought also encountered critiques from emerging psychological paradigms that underscored the limitations of a purely stimulus-response framework for understanding complex emotional processes. These critiques, while challenging, stimulated a reconsideration of foundational assumptions, sparking a wave of introspection and innovation within the behaviorist camp.

Ultimately, the post-war era stands as a pivotal chapter in the chronicles of emotional conditioning, heralding an era of unparalleled exploration, diversification, and integration. An era where the seeds sown in the early days of behaviorism blossomed into a vibrant tapestry of scientific inquiry, technological advancement, and therapeutic innovation.

Critiques and Challenges from Emerging Psychological Paradigms

As emotional conditioning gained prominence in the post-war era, it inevitably faced critiques and challenges from emerging psychological paradigms. One of the major criticisms stemmed from the growing influence of cognitive psychology, which emphasized the role of mental processes such as perception, attention, and memory in shaping behavior. Critics argued that emotional conditioning, with its sole focus on observable behaviors, overlooked the interplay between cognition and emotion. This led to debates about the necessity of incorporating cognitive elements into the traditional behaviorist framework, sparking a paradigmatic shift within the field. Additionally, humanistic psychology presented an alternative perspective that challenged the reductionist nature of behaviorism. Humanistic psychologists highlighted the importance of individual subjective experiences, free will, and self-actualization, which stood in stark contrast to the deterministic principles of emotional conditioning. These critiques raised fundamental questions about the nature of human behavior and experience, necessitating a reevaluation of the existing paradigms. Furthermore, advancements in neuroscience and psychopharmacology introduced new dimensions to the study of emotions and behaviors, offering biological explanations for emotional responses that transcended the confines of environmental stimuli. This posed a formidable challenge to the purely environmental determinism espoused by emotional conditioning, leading to heated discussions about the relative contributions of genetics, neurobiology, and environment to emotional development. The advent of evolutionary psychology also posed significant challenges to the prevailing notions of emotional conditioning by emphasizing the adaptive functions of emotions in human survival and reproduction. By implicating evolutionary forces in emotional processes, this paradigm shed light on the ancient origins of certain emotional responses, casting doubts on the exclusivity of learned associations as proposed by emotional conditioning. Moreover, social and cultural psychology raised pertinent questions about the cross-cultural applicability of emotional conditioning, hinting at the potential variability of emotional responses across diverse societal contexts. As such, the discipline faced the compelling task of reconciling these critiques and integrating insights from disparate psychological perspectives into a more comprehensive framework.

Integration into Broader Psychological Frameworks

The integration of emotional conditioning into broader psychological frameworks has been an intriguing and complex process, marked by significant contributions and debates within the field. As behaviorism gradually evolved and diversified, emotional conditioning found itself woven into the fabric of psychological research and practice in various ways. One prominent avenue of integration has been through the lens of cognitive psychology, where the interplay between conditioning processes and higher-order cognitive functions has sparked extensive exploration. This has led to a deeper understanding of how emotions are not only classically conditioned but also influenced by cognitive appraisals, expectations, and beliefs. The incorporation of emotional conditioning principles into cognitive-behavioral therapies has yielded promising results, underscoring the practical implications of this integration. Furthermore, the assimilation of emotional conditioning into developmental psychology has shed light on the impact of early experiences on emotional regulation and psychopathology. Researchers have delved into the mechanisms through which conditioning shapes emotional development, offering valuable insights into childhood disorders and interventions. Another avenue of integration has been through the burgeoning field of affective neuroscience, where advances in brain imaging techniques have provided compelling evidence of the neural substrates underlying conditioned emotional responses. This interdisciplinary approach has deepened our comprehension of the neurobiological underpinnings of emotional conditioning, elucidating the interplay between genetic predispositions, environmental factors, and learning processes. Moreover, evolutionary psychology has contributed to the integration of emotional conditioning by examining its adaptive significance across species and cultures. By situating emotional conditioning within the framework of natural selection and reproductive fitness, researchers have elucidated the adaptive value of acquiring and expressing emotional responses to salient stimuli. This multifaceted integration into broader psychological frameworks underscores the far-reaching implications and applications of emotional conditioning across diverse domains of psychological inquiry. As we continue to unravel the complexities of human emotion and behavior, this integration will undoubtedly play a pivotal role in shaping our understanding of psychological phenomena and informing evidence-based interventions.

Legacy of Early Emotional Conditioning in Contemporary Research

The profound impact of early emotional conditioning on our understanding of human behavior and emotion is evident in its continued relevance and influence on modern psychological frameworks. This legacy is particularly pronounced in contemporary research, where principles derived from classical and operant conditioning continue to inform and enrich empirical studies across diverse domains of psychological inquiry.

One key aspect of the legacy of early emotional conditioning lies in its contribution to the understanding of anxiety disorders and phobias. By examining the mechanisms underlying emotional conditioning, researchers have been able to elucidate the development and maintenance of maladaptive emotional responses, providing valuable insights into effective therapeutic interventions. Furthermore, advancements in cognitive-behavioral therapies have drawn extensively from the principles of emotional conditioning, emphasizing the role of learned associations in perpetuating dysfunctional emotional states. Through rigorous empirical investigation, contemporary researchers have expanded upon the foundational work of behaviorists to develop sophisticated models of emotional learning, shedding light on the interplay between cognition, emotion, and behavior.

The legacy of early emotional conditioning extends beyond clinical psychology, permeating diverse fields such as developmental psychology and social neuroscience. Studies exploring the role of emotional conditioning in childhood development have underscored the influence of early emotional experiences on later psychological functioning. These inquiries have not only deepened our understanding of emotional development but have also prompted the refinement of intervention strategies aimed at promoting healthy socio-emotional growth in children and adolescents.

In the sphere of social neuroscience, investigations into the neural substrates of emotional conditioning have yielded invaluable insights into the underlying neurobiological processes that govern adaptive and maladaptive emotional responses. Utilizing advanced neuroimaging techniques, contemporary researchers have delineated the neural circuits implicated in emotional memory and extinction, offering nuanced understanding of neural plasticity in the context of emotional learning. Such findings hold profound implications for the design of targeted interventions in clinical settings, underpinning the development of neurocognitive interventions tailored to ameliorate pathological emotional states.

The legacy of early emotional conditioning resonates strongly with contemporary behavioral research, permeating fields such as addiction psychology and organizational behavior. By scrutinizing the role of associative learning in addictive behaviors, researchers have elucidated the mechanisms by which conditioned cues precipitate craving and relapse, informing the design of comprehensive treatment approaches. Similarly, in organizational behavior, the principles of emotional conditioning have informed nuanced investigations into employee motivation, affective contagion, and organizational culture, offering fertile ground for understanding the impact of environmental stimuli on affective states and behavioral outcomes.

JOHN B. WATSON'S LIFE AND CAREER

Early Life and Education

John Broadus Watson was born on January 9, 1878 in Travelers Rest, South Carolina. His father, Pickens Butler Watson, was a farmer and itinerant carpenter, while his mother, Emma Kesiah Watson, was a religious and pious woman who greatly influenced John's early life. Growing up on a farm, young Watson developed a strong work ethic and a deep appreciation for the natural world. Despite the family's modest means, education was highly valued, and Watson's parents instilled in him the importance of learning and academic achievement. This nurturing environment laid the foundation for his future intellectual pursuits. As a precocious child, Watson demonstrated an insatiable curiosity about the world around him, often quizzing his elders with questions about nature, animals, and human behavior. His formative years in the rural South provided him with a firsthand understanding of the complexities of human interactions within a predominantly agricultural society. Watson's early education was largely informal, with limited access to formal schooling. However, his innate intellect and thirst for knowledge soon became evident, prompting his family to seek out educational opportunities for him. At the age of 16, he enrolled at Furman University, where he studied philosophy, English, and animal behavior, laying the groundwork for his future contributions to the field of psychology. Influenced by the teachings of renowned psychologist and philosopher John Dewey, Watson developed an interest in the study of human behavior and its underlying mechanisms. He recognized the profound impact that environmental factors had on shaping individual conduct and psychology and began to formulate his groundbreaking theories. It was during this period that he established himself as a diligent student and a fervent advocate for the empirical examination of human behavior.

Influences and Inspirations

John B. Watson's lifelong intellectual curiosity and passion for psychology were influenced by a myriad of factors, shaping his perspectives and fueling his innovative ideas. During his formative years, Watson was deeply impacted by the works of renowned psychologists such as Ivan Pavlov, William James, and Sigmund Freud. Their profound investigations into human behavior and the workings of the mind captivated Watson and served as the catalyst for his relentless pursuit of understanding the complexities of the human psyche. The early 20th century was a time of significant scientific and philosophical shifts, and Watson found himself immersed in this transformative period, drawing inspiration from the burgeoning fields of physiology, neurology, and experimental psychology. As he delved into the wealth of research and theories emerging at the time, Watson was profoundly influenced by the ideas of determinism and empiricism, which became foundational pillars in his own psychological framework. Furthermore, Watson's personal experiences and encounters also played a pivotal role in shaping his intellectual journey. His interactions with mentors, colleagues, and even adversaries deeply impacted his perspectives, pushing him to challenge existing paradigms and cultivate his unique approach to the study of behavior. Additionally, the socio-cultural milieu of the era, marked by rapid industrialization and urbanization, provided a rich backdrop against which Watson developed his theories, seeking to unravel the mysteries of human behavior amidst the evolving landscape of modernity.

Academic Pursuits and Breakthroughs

Delving into the sphere of academic scholarship, Watson embarked on an intellectual journey that would come to define his career. His pioneering work in the field of behavioral psychology revolutionized the understanding of human behavior and laid the groundwork for subsequent research and developments in the discipline.

Watson's pursuit of academically rigorous inquiries led him to focus on the empirical study of behavior and the exploration of observable phenomena. By prioritizing a scientific approach to psychology, he sought to unravel the complexities of human behavior through systematic observation and experimentation. This determination to apply scientific principles to the study of psychological processes marked a watershed moment in the evolution of psychological scholarship.

Amidst his academic pursuits, Watson achieved a series of groundbreaking breakthroughs that reshaped the landscape of psychology. One such monumental breakthrough was his conceptualization and establishment of the theory of classical conditioning, which posited that behaviors could be learned through the association of stimuli. This innovative paradigm not only provided a profound insight into the mechanisms underlying behavioral acquisition but also laid the foundation for subsequent advancements in the study of learning and behavior.

Watson's application of objective methodologies and rigorous standards in his research exemplified his commitment to advancing psychological science. His influential studies, including the infamous Little Albert experiment, showcased his ability to construct experiments that yielded invaluable insights into the nature of human behavior. Through these endeavors, he pioneered a new era of experimental psychology, setting a benchmark for methodological rigor and precision that reverberated throughout the field.

Beyond the confines of traditional academic pursuits, Watson's charismatic and dynamic approach to scholarship inspired a generation of psychologists to embrace the empirical rigor and objectivity that he championed. His unwavering dedication to advancing the boundaries of knowledge in behavioral psychology left an indelible mark on the discipline and solidified his legacy as a preeminent figure in the history of psychology.

Foundational Role in Behavioral Psychology

In the annals of psychological history, John B. Watson's foundational role in behavioral psychology remains indisputable. His revolutionary ideas and pioneering experiments mark a transformative juncture in the evolution of psychological theory and practice. Watson's unwavering commitment to rigorously empirical investigation led him to challenge prevailing introspective methods and laid the groundwork for the development of behaviorism as a distinct school of thought within psychology. Central to his foundational role was the deliberate departure from the traditional focus on internal mental processes and the espousal of a scientific approach that prioritized observable behaviors as the primary subject of psychological inquiry. This intellectual shift irreversibly transformed the landscape of psychology and firmly established behaviorism as a dominant paradigm for generations to come. At the heart of Watson's foundational role in behavioral psychology lies the articulation of a systematic framework for understanding human behavior through the lens of environmental stimuli and learned responses. His emphasis on objective, measurable phenomena resonated deeply within the scientific community, fostering a paradigmatic shift towards a more empirical and verifiable approach to studying human behavior. Furthermore, Watson's influential exposition of behaviorism laid the theoretical groundwork for subsequent advancements in fields such as operant conditioning and social learning theory, exerting a profound and enduring influence on the broader discipline of psychology. Beyond mere theoretical contributions, Watson's foundational role also manifested in the practical applications of behaviorist principles to diverse domains such as education, clinical intervention, and advertising. His deliberate emphasis on the environmental determinants of behavior fostered a paradigm shift, empowering psychologists to intervene directly in shaping and modifying human behavior by manipulating environmental contingencies. As a result, Watson's legacy transcends the confines of academic discourse, permeating into the fabric of societal practices and cultural norms.

Major Contributions to Psychological Research

Through his pioneering work, Watson laid the groundwork for the founding principles of behaviorism, a school of thought that would significantly influence psychology for decades to come. One of his most significant contributions was the emphasis on observable behavior as a critical component of psychological study, shifting the focus away from the then-dominant introspective methods associated with structuralism and functionalism. This redirection of attention towards overt actions and reactions revolutionized the field, stimulating an empirical approach to understanding human behavior. Watson's dedication to experimental methodology, particularly in the domain of conditioning, was instrumental in establishing the scientific rigor and objectivity that continues to underpin contemporary psychological inquiry. His influential 'Little Albert' experiment, where he demonstrated how fear could be conditioned in a young child, remains emblematic of his groundbreaking research. Furthermore, Watson's articulation of the concept of learned emotional responses and the mechanisms by which they are acquired laid the groundwork for a more comprehensive understanding of human behavior and emotion. Moreover, Watson's advocacy for applying principles of behaviorism in practical areas such as education and advertising inspired an entire generation of researchers and practitioners to integrate psychological insights into real-world contexts. By highlighting the importance of environmental factors in shaping behavior and personality, Watson also catalyzed a paradigm shift in the study of developmental psychology, contributing significantly to a deeper comprehension of the influences that mold individuals across their lifespan. His influence reverberates in the neuroscientific explorations of learning, memory, and emotion, as well as in the domains of clinical and counseling psychology, underscoring the relevance of his work.

Controversies and Ethical Considerations

One of the most prominent ethical debates surrounding Watson's research pertains to his famous Little Albert experiment. This experiment involved conditioning a young child to fear a white rat by pairing its presence with a loud, jarring noise. Critics have argued that this study raised significant ethical concerns regarding the treatment of the child and the long-term psychological impact of the conditioning. Furthermore, there are questions about the adequacy of consent and whether the child's parents were fully informed about the nature and potential consequences of the study. These ethical considerations continue to provoke debate among psychologists, ethicists, and researchers. Another controversy associated with Watson's work relates to his transition from academia to the world of advertising. His move into the advertising industry marked a departure from the traditional confines of academic research and raised questions about potential conflicts of interest and the commodification of psychological knowledge for commercial gain. Critics raised concerns about the application of behavioral principles to marketing and the ethical implications of manipulating consumer behavior. Additionally, Watson's public persona and controversial personal life, including his highly publicized affair and divorce, also sparked ethical discussions within the academic community. The intertwining of personal conduct and professional contributions led to debates about the ethical responsibilities of influential figures in the field of psychology.

Transition from Academia to Advertising

After the contentious period marked by controversies and ethical considerations, John B. Watson underwent a significant transition in his career, moving away from academia into the domain of advertising. This shift was a pivotal moment in Watson's life as it not only redirected his professional trajectory but also sparked debates about the ethical implications of applying psychological principles in the sphere of marketing and consumer behavior.

Following his departure from the academic sphere, Watson delved into the world of advertising, bringing his expertise in behavioral psychology to bear on the strategies and tactics employed by businesses seeking to influence consumer preferences. His groundbreaking contributions in this arena fundamentally transformed the landscape of advertising and consumer research, paving the way for the widespread adoption of psychologically informed marketing practices.

Watson's foray into advertising was characterized by the application of behavioral theories to understand and manipulate consumer behavior. Drawing on his deep understanding of human psychology, Watson introduced innovative methods for crafting persuasive advertising messages and designing compelling campaigns that resonated with the target audience's motivations and desires. By leveraging principles of emotional conditioning and behavior modification, Watson revolutionized the way products and services were marketed, ushering in a new era of strategic advertising that harnessed the power of psychological insights.

However, this transition was not without its share of controversy. Critics raised ethical concerns about the use of psychological tactics to manipulate consumer behavior and questioned the moral implications of exploiting individuals' subconscious triggers for commercial gain. Watson's involvement in advertising prompted fervent discussions within the academic community and the broader public, fueling debates about the boundaries of ethical advertising practices and the responsible application of psychological knowledge in the commercial domain.

Watson's transition from academia to advertising sparked reflection on the broader impact of psychology on society, underscoring the far-reaching influence of psychological principles beyond traditional academic settings. His role in shaping the advertising landscape underscored the interconnectedness of psychology, business, and consumer culture, stimulating ongoing deliberations about the ethical dimensions of leveraging psychological insights in the pursuit of commercial objectives.

Ultimately, Watson's shift from academia to advertising left an indelible mark on the fields of psychology and marketing, forever altering the way in which consumer behavior was understood and influenced. His legacy in the sphere of advertising continues to provoke deep contemplation regarding the responsible and ethical application of psychological knowledge in the dynamic arena of commerce and consumerism.

Lasting Impact on Behaviorism

Watson's emphasis on observable behavior as a fundamental element in the study of human psychology revolutionized the way we understand and approach human behavior and laid the groundwork for the behaviorist movement.

One of the key contributions to behaviorism was the development of the theory of classical conditioning, which provided a systematic framework for understanding how environmental stimuli can elicit conditioned responses. This foundational concept not only facilitated empirical research but also inspired subsequent generations of psychologists to delve deeper into the mechanisms underlying behavioral conditioning.

Watson's advocacy for the rigorous application of scientific methods in studying human behavior set a high standard for psychological research. His insistence on objective measurement and experimentation helped to establish behaviorism as a rigorously empirical science, earning it credibility and respect within the academic community. By emphasizing the importance of observable and measurable phenomena, Watson's approach promoted an evidence-based foundation for psychological inquiry that continues to shape the discipline today.

Additionally, Watson's work paved the way for the broader acceptance of behaviorism as a significant theoretical perspective in psychology. By highlighting the influence of environmental factors on behavior and the potential for behavior modification through conditioning, Watson's teachings sparked widespread interest and exploration of these ideas in various domains such as education, therapy, and even advertising. This impact continues to resonate across diverse fields, demonstrating the relevance of behaviorist principles.

Watson's commitment to empiricism and emphasis on environmental determinants of behavior catalyzed advancements in applied behavior analysis and behavioral therapies. His legacy can be seen in the development of interventions aimed at addressing maladaptive behaviors and promoting positive behavioral change, underscoring the practical implications of his theoretical framework.

CORE PRINCIPLES OF WATSONIAN PSYCHOLOGY

Behaviorism - The Foundational Assumptions

1. Fundamental Principles:

Behaviorism is grounded in several fundamental principles that form the basis of this psychological approach. At its core, behaviorism emphasizes the importance of observable behavior as the primary focus of study, advocating for a scientific and objective analysis of human actions and reactions. This perspective rejects the exploration of internal mental states or subjective experiences, instead prioritizing the external stimuli that elicit specific responses. One of the key principles of behaviorism is the concept of conditioning, which highlights the influence of environmental factors in shaping behaviors. This involves the process of learning through associations, whereby individuals adapt their responses based on past experiences and the reinforcement or punishment received. Furthermore, behaviorism underscores the significance of environmental determinism, suggesting that behavior is primarily influenced by external factors rather than inherent traits. This principle aligns with the belief that individuals' actions are malleable and can be modified through intentional manipulation of their surroundings. Another essential tenet of behaviorism is the emphasis on empiricism and experimentation, emphasizing the application of rigorous scientific methods to study behavior and validate theories. Through systematic observation and controlled experiments, behaviorists seek to identify consistent patterns and principles underlying human behavior, contributing to the establishment of empirically-supported principles. Additionally, behaviorism encompasses the principles of generalization and discrimination, wherein learned behaviors can be applied to similar stimuli or differentiated from others, reflecting the adaptive nature of conditioned responses. The rejection of introspection and reliance on empirical evidence further distinguish behaviorism's fundamental principles, aligning with its commitment to objectivity and replicability in psychological research. Overall, these foundational principles of behaviorism shape its distinct perspective on human behavior, highlighting the systematic study of observable actions, the influence of environmental stimuli, and the role of learning and adaptation in shaping behavior.

2. Distinction from Other Psychological Approaches:

Behaviorism, as a psychological approach, distinguishes itself significantly from other schools of thought prevalent in the field. Traditional psychology, rooted in introspection and the study of internal mental states, contrasts sharply with behaviorism's focus on observable behavior. While psychoanalysis delves into subconscious motivations and personality structures, behaviorism emphasizes the influence of the external environment on shaping human actions and reactions. Additionally, cognitive psychology, which emerged later, revolves around mental processes such as perception, attention, and memory, whereas behaviorism directs attention to the responses elicited by external stimuli and the process of learning through reinforcement and conditioning.

One of the notable distinctions lies in behaviorism's rejection of the concept of introspection and subjective experiences. While previous branches of psychology relied heavily on individuals' self-reporting and interpretation of their inner thoughts and emotions, behaviorism prioritizes empirical observation and measurable behaviors. This shift towards objective, quantifiable data sets behaviorism apart from its predecessors, marking a clear departure from the subjective nature of earlier psychological approaches.

Behaviorism's emphasis on environmental determinants of behavior sets it apart from the focus on innate qualities and inner dispositions prominent in other psychological paradigms. Unlike psychodynamic theories that emphasize inherent drives and unconscious forces, behaviorism stresses the impact of external stimuli and reinforcement in shaping behavior. This focus on the role of the environment in determining behavioral responses establishes behaviorism as a distinctive and influential psychological framework.

Another differentiation arises in behaviorism's practical applications and relevance in various fields, including education, therapy, and organizational behavior management. By emphasizing the significance of learning and conditioning in molding behavior, behaviorism has contributed to the development of effective teaching methods, behavior modification techniques, and interventions for addressing maladaptive behavior patterns. This practical utility further delineates behaviorism from other theoretical perspectives within psychology.

3. The Role of Observational Behavior:

Observational behavior serves as a core tenet that shapes the understanding of learning and adaptation. This aspect of behaviorism emphasizes the significance of individuals witnessing and imitating the actions of others, influencing their own behavioral patterns. Derived from the influential work of behaviorist theorist Albert Bandura, observational behavior has been regarded as a crucial mechanism for acquiring new skills, attitudes, and behaviors. Bandura's seminal 'Social Learning Theory' underscores the notion that individuals, particularly children, learn not only through direct reinforcement but also through observing the behaviors of others and the consequences associated with those behaviors.

At the heart of observational behavior lies the concept of modeling, where individuals observe the actions of others, including peers, parents, or influential figures, and subsequently emulate these actions. Through this process of modeling, individuals internalize observed behaviors, which may then influence their own conduct. Moreover, observational behavior extends beyond simple mimicry to encompass complex cognitive processes, such as attention, retention, reproduction, and motivation. This multifaceted approach emphasizes the active cognitive engagement of individuals during observational learning, highlighting the interplay between external stimuli and internal mental processes.

Observational behavior transcends the confines of individual experiences, as it encompasses cultural transmission and the dissemination of societal norms and values. In diverse cultural settings, observational behavior serves as a key mechanism for transmitting customs, traditions, and social norms across generations. By observing and mirroring the behaviors of cultural models, individuals assimilate cultural practices, rituals, and beliefs, contributing to the perpetuation and evolution of collective societal norms.

The impact of observational behavior is pervasive, extending to various domains such as education, media influence, and interpersonal interactions. In educational settings, the demonstration of desired behaviors by teachers and peers can significantly influence students' learning and socialization. Similarly, the media's representation of role models and influential figures can shape public behavior and societal trends. Additionally, within interpersonal dynamics, observational learning molds social behavior, interpersonal relationships, and group dynamics, exemplifying the far-reaching implications of this behavioral mechanism.

4. The Exclusion of Internal Mental States:

Behaviorism has long been characterized by its deliberate exclusion of internal mental states from its scope of study. This fundamental aspect reflects the behaviorist belief that only observable behaviors can be reliably studied and measured, whereas internal mental processes remain subjective and elusive. The exclusion of internal mental states signifies a departure from introspective methods championed by earlier schools of psychology and asserts the primacy of studying behavior in response to external stimuli.

Central to this exclusion is the behaviorist emphasis on the importance of environmental determinants in shaping an individual's actions and reactions. Behaviorists argue that focusing on internal mental states leads to speculation and unverifiable interpretations, deviating from the scientific rigor that underpins their methodology. Instead, behaviorists advocate for the rigorous observation and analysis of how an individual's environment influences their behavioral responses, emphasizing the predictability and control of behavior through the manipulation of environmental variables.

Critics have challenged behaviorism's exclusion of internal mental states, arguing that it neglects the rich complexity of human cognition and emotion. They contend that cognitive processes, such as memory, language, and problem-solving, play crucial roles in understanding human behavior, and dismissing their significance limits the comprehensive comprehension of human nature. In response, contemporary behaviorism has evolved to integrate cognitive principles while maintaining its focus on observable behavior, giving rise to the cognitive-behavioral approach that acknowledges the interplay between overt behavior and underlying mental processes.

Behaviorism's exclusion of internal mental states has implications for areas beyond individual psychology, including social, cultural, and societal dynamics. By prioritizing observable behavior, behaviorism directs attention to the influence of external factors, highlighting the impact of environmental conditions, social reinforcement, and cultural norms on human behavior. This perspective underscores the potential for societal intervention and change through the manipulation of environmental contingencies, offering insights into behavior modification and social engineering.

5. The Mechanisms of Learning and Adaptation:

The mechanisms of learning and adaptation lie at the heart of behaviorism, encompassing a complex interplay of environmental stimuli and behavioral responses. Central to this exploration is the concept of conditioning, a fundamental mechanism through which behaviorists seek to explain the acquisition and modification of behavior. Classical conditioning, as pioneered by Ivan Pavlov and further developed by John B. Watson, outlines how associations between stimuli and responses are formed through repeated pairings, leading to learned behavioral reactions. Meanwhile, operant conditioning, elucidated by B.F. Skinner, focuses on the role of consequences in shaping behavior, presenting a comprehensive framework for understanding how reinforcement and punishment influence the likelihood of specific behaviors occurring in the future. Furthermore, the concept of generalization is expounded upon, illuminating how individuals may extend learned responses to similar stimuli, thus broadening the applicability of acquired behaviors. Conversely, the complementary process of discrimination is explored, illustrating how individuals learn to differentiate between distinct stimuli and appropriately modify their responses accordingly. The intertwining of these principles creates a rich tapestry of learning and adaptation, shaping the behavioral landscape within a behaviorist framework. Additionally, considerations are given to the phenomena of spontaneous recovery, where previously extinguished responses re-emerge, shedding light on the intricacies of behavioral maintenance.

6. Scientific Approach to Behavior Analysis:

Behavior analysis, as a scientific approach, encompasses the systematic study of observable behavior and the environmental factors that influence it. This thorough examination involves the precise measurement and experimental manipulation of behavior to uncover consistent patterns and principles. Through rigorous experimentation and observation, behavior analysts strive to identify the underlying mechanisms that control behavior and determine how these behaviors are impacted by various stimuli and consequences. Central to behavior analysis is the application of objective and replicable research methodologies, such as controlled experiments and direct observation, to investigate and understand behavior in diverse contexts and populations.

A critical element of the scientific approach to behavior analysis is the emphasis on empirical evidence and the rejection of speculative interpretations or unsubstantiated theories. By adhering to this empirical foundation, behavior analysts can maintain an objective stance that fosters credibility and reliability in their findings and conclusions. Furthermore, the meticulous collection and analysis of quantitative data allow for the establishment of reliable predictive relationships between antecedents, behaviors, and consequences, thus forming the basis for informed interventions and applications.

In addition, the scientific approach to behavior analysis prioritizes the precise operational definition of target behaviors and the identification of relevant environmental variables that shape or maintain these behaviors. This process involves breaking down complex behaviors into specific, measurable components and systematically analyzing the functional relationships between stimuli and responses. Through this analytical lens, behavior analysts can develop comprehensive interventions and behavior modification programs that directly target and address the underlying causes of certain behaviors, ultimately leading to more effective and sustainable outcomes.

The scientific rigor inherent in behavior analysis allows for the continuous refinement and improvement of behavioral interventions and assessment tools through ongoing research and clinical application. By integrating new insights and empirical findings into practice, behavior analysts can enhance the effectiveness and precision of their interventions, ensuring that their work remains aligned with the latest advancements in the field.

Overall, the scientific approach to behavior analysis serves as the cornerstone of evidence-based practices and interventions, providing a systematic framework for understanding, assessing, and modifying behavior in a wide range of settings and populations.

7. Critiques from the Psychological Community:

The advent of behaviorism brought about significant transformation in the field of psychology, but it was not immune to critique from within the psychological community. One prominent critique revolves around the oversimplification of human behavior. Behaviorism's exclusive focus on observable behaviors led to an oversight of the complex cognitive processes that underpin human actions. Critics argue that by neglecting internal mental states, behaviorism fails to provide a comprehensive understanding of the human experience, thereby limiting its explanatory power. Moreover, behaviorism's deterministic view of behavior as strictly determined by environmental stimuli has been contested, with critics asserting that it overlooks the influence of individual agency and free will. The reductionist nature of behaviorism, which reduces all behavior to learned responses, has also been a point of contention. Critics argue that this approach fails to account for the rich tapestry of human experiences, emotions, and motivations that cannot be solely attributed to conditioning and reinforcement. Additionally, the ethical implications of behaviorism's emphasis on behavior modification through conditioning have sparked concerns within the psychological community. The use of behavioral techniques in various applications, such as advertising and persuasion, has raised ethical dilemmas regarding individual autonomy and manipulation. Furthermore, some critics argue that behaviorism's rejection of introspection and subjective experiences diminishes the holistic understanding of human behavior. By disregarding the internal landscape of thoughts, emotions, and perceptions, behaviorism is perceived as offering an incomplete portrayal of human psychology. The disregard for evolutionary and biological influences on behavior is another facet that has drawn criticism. Critics contend that behaviorism's exclusive emphasis on environmental determinants neglects the intrinsic role of genetics, evolutionary history, and neurobiology in shaping behavior. This oversight potentially limits the breadth of psychological understanding.

8. Influence on Modern Psychology:

Despite the critiques and controversies that have arisen, behaviorism continues to play a vital role in contemporary psychological research and practice. One of the most notable influences of behaviorism is its emphasis on empirical evidence and scientific methodology. The commitment to observable and measurable phenomena has permeated modern psychological approaches, contributing to the rigorous and systematic study of human behavior.

Behaviorism's focus on the environmental determinants of behavior has significantly shaped contemporary therapeutic interventions. The principles of behaviorism have been integrated into various forms of behavioral therapy, such as cognitive-behavioral therapy (CBT), which remains one of the most widely practiced and effective approaches in clinical psychology. Through the application of behaviorist principles, therapists can address maladaptive behaviors and cognitions by modifying environmental stimuli and reinforcing more adaptive patterns.

Behaviorism's conception of learning as a process of conditioning has left an indelible mark on educational psychology. The application of behaviorist principles in the design of instructional materials and teaching methods has greatly influenced the field of education, leading to the development of evidence-based strategies for enhancing learning outcomes. By understanding how behavioral responses are shaped through reinforcement and extinction, educators have been able to refine pedagogical techniques to optimize student engagement and motivation.

In addition, behaviorism's rejection of mentalistic explanations and its insistence on objective and observable behaviors have catalyzed advancements in experimental psychology, particularly in the domain of animal behavior research. The empirical rigor and precise measurement techniques advocated by behaviorism have facilitated groundbreaking studies on topics ranging from operant conditioning to the neurobiological underpinnings of behavior. This has not only deepened our understanding of animal cognition and behavior but has also provided valuable insights into human behavior, serving as a bridge between experimental psychology and behavioral neuroscience.

Ultimately, the influence of behaviorism on modern psychology manifests in its pervasive impact across diverse domains, including clinical practice, education, and research. While the field of psychology has evolved and incorporated perspectives from other theoretical frameworks, the foundational principles and methodologies championed by behaviorism endure as integral components of the discipline, underscoring its relevance and significance.

Objective Study of Behavior

1. Historical Context and the Shift from Introspection:

In the late 19th and early 20th centuries, psychology underwent a paradigm shift as it transitioned from introspective methods of study to an objective analysis of behavior. This transition was driven by a desire to establish psychology as a scientific discipline with observable, measurable phenomena at its core. The rejection of introspection as a reliable method for understanding mental processes led to a fundamental reevaluation of the field, setting the stage for the rise of behaviorism and objective behavior analysis. One of the driving forces behind this shift was the skepticism surrounding the subjective nature of introspection, which lacked replicability and often resulted in conflicting interpretations among researchers. Additionally, the advent of new experimental techniques and advancements in technology paved the way for a more empirical approach to studying human behavior. The works of psychologists such as Wilhelm Wundt, Edward Titchener, and William James mark the pivotal period during which the dominance of introspection started to wane, making room for the emergence of objectivity as the hallmark of psychological inquiry. This historical context illuminates the intellectual climate that precipitated the transition from the subjective study of consciousness to the objective examination of behavior, laying the groundwork for the transformative developments that followed.

2. Methodological Approaches in Behavior Observation:

In the study of behavior, employing methodological approaches in observation is vital for ensuring the validity and accuracy of findings. One prominent approach is naturalistic observation, where researchers observe subjects in their natural environments without interference. This method allows for an authentic representation of behavior but may present challenges in terms of control and standardization. Alternatively, controlled observation involves creating specific settings or scenarios to elicit targeted behaviors, providing researchers with more controlled conditions for observation and analysis.

Another methodological approach is participant observation, wherein the researcher becomes actively involved in the setting being studied. This approach allows for a deeper understanding of the context and nuances of behavior but may introduce biases due to the researcher's involvement. On the other hand, non-participant observation involves observing behavior from a distance, minimizing potential influence on the subjects' actions.

Systematic observation involves the structured recording of behavior using predefined categories and coding schemes, enabling quantitative analysis of behavioral patterns. Video recording and analysis have become integral in behavior observation, allowing for precise scrutiny, as well as the review and evaluation of behaviors through slow-motion and repeated observations.

Technological advancements have given rise to innovative methods of behavior observation, such as eye-tracking technology, which provides insights into visual attention and gaze behaviors.

Additionally, physiological measures like electroencephalography (EEG) and functional magnetic resonance imaging (fMRI) enable researchers to correlate behavior with underlying neural activity, offering a deeper understanding of the mechanisms driving behavior.

Ethical considerations in behavior observation are paramount, necessitating the establishment of protocols to protect the rights and well-being of participants. Informed consent, confidentiality, and debriefing procedures should be meticulously addressed in the design and execution of behavior observation studies to uphold ethical standards.

3. Role of Experimentation in Studying Behavior:

By systematically manipulating variables and measuring resulting behavioral responses, researchers can unravel complex patterns and causal relationships, shedding light on the underlying mechanisms governing human and animal behavior. The process of experimentation allows for the control of extraneous influences, enabling researchers to isolate specific factors contributing to observed behaviors.

In behavioral studies, experiments provide a means to test hypotheses and theories, offering empirical evidence to support or refute proposed explanations. Through carefully designed experimental protocols, researchers can investigate a wide range of behavioral phenomena, from simple reflexes to intricate cognitive processes. This systematic approach fosters the accumulation of reliable data, essential for building a comprehensive understanding of behavior.

Experimental designs in behavior research often involve the manipulation of independent variables, such as environmental stimuli or task conditions, and the subsequent observation of resulting changes in dependent variables, i.e., behavioral responses. These controlled manipulations allow researchers to establish cause-and-effect relationships, illuminating the interplay between environmental factors and behavior.

Experimentation in behavior study facilitates the exploration of individual differences and developmental trajectories. By exposing participants to various experimental conditions, researchers can discern how different individuals respond to the same stimuli, highlighting the nuanced nature of behavioral variability. Moreover, longitudinal experimental designs enable scientists to track behavioral changes over time, unveiling the dynamic nature of behavioral development.

Technological advancements have significantly enhanced the precision and scope of behavioral experimentation. Sophisticated measurement tools, such as eye-tracking devices, electroencephalography (EEG) machines, and functional magnetic resonance imaging (fMRI) scanners, provide unprecedented insights into neural correlates of behavior and cognition. Additionally, advancements in data analytics and computational modeling empower researchers to analyze complex behavioral datasets, unveiling intricate patterns and associations.

4. Technology and Tools for Measurement:

Technological advancements have revolutionized the field of behavioral research by providing researchers with sophisticated tools for measurement and analysis. One such tool is the actigraphy monitor, a wrist-worn device that measures movement and rest cycles over extended periods. This technology enables researchers to gather objective data on sleep patterns, physical activity, and circadian rhythms, offering valuable insights into behavioral patterns. Additionally, the use of functional magnetic resonance imaging (fMRI) has allowed neuroscientists to correlate specific behaviors with brain activity, shedding light on the neural mechanisms underlying behavior. The advancement of video tracking systems has also been instrumental in capturing and quantifying complex behaviors, facilitating detailed analyses that were previously unattainable. Furthermore, the development of wearable biosensors has enabled continuous monitoring of physiological parameters such as heart rate variability, skin conductance, and body temperature, providing real-time data on emotional and stress responses. In addition, eye-tracking technology has enhanced our understanding of visual attention and gaze patterns, offering valuable information about cognitive processes and decision-making. Moreover, the application of virtual reality simulations has enabled researchers to create controlled environments to study behavior in diverse contexts, offering a unique perspective on human interactions and responses. Furthermore, advancements in machine learning algorithms have facilitated automated analysis of large-scale behavioral data, allowing for the detection of subtle patterns and trends that may have previously gone unnoticed. These technologies have not only expanded the scope of behavioral research but have also enhanced the reliability and validity of measurements, enabling more precise and comprehensive investigations into human behavior.

5. Reliability and Validity in Behavioral Research:

Reliability and validity are crucial aspects in ensuring the credibility and robustness of behavioral research. Reliability refers to the consistency and stability of measurement over time, whereas validity pertains to the accuracy and meaningfulness of the inferences drawn from the measurements. In the context of behavioral research, establishing both reliability and validity is essential to ensure that the findings and conclusions are trustworthy and applicable.

When it comes to reliability in behavioral research, researchers strive to achieve consistency in their measurements. This entails ensuring that the same results would be obtained if the study were to be repeated under similar conditions. Several methods can be employed to assess reliability, such as test-retest reliability, inter-rater reliability, and internal consistency. For instance, in observational studies, inter-rater reliability is particularly crucial, as it measures the degree of agreement among different observers assessing the same behavior, thereby ensuring that the observations are consistent and not influenced by individual biases.

On the other hand, validity concerns the extent to which a particular measure or instrument accurately captures the construct or concept it aims to assess. In behavioral research, various types of validity need to be considered, including content validity, criterion validity, and construct validity. Content validity ensures that the measurement comprehensively covers all aspects of the intended construct, while criterion validity assesses how well the measure predicts or correlates with other established criteria. Meanwhile, construct validity evaluates the extent to which the measure assesses the theoretical construct it purports to measure.

Challenges may arise in achieving reliability and validity in behavioral research, particularly due to the complexity and variability of human behavior. Factors such as participant compliance, environmental influences, and situational factors can impact the reliability and validity of measurements. Additionally, the selection and design of measurement tools and methodologies can influence the extent to which reliability and validity are established. Therefore, researchers need to rigorously consider these challenges and employ appropriate strategies to enhance reliability and validity in their studies. Utilizing multiple measures, incorporating feedback and pilot testing, and employing standardized protocols are some approaches utilized to address these challenges.

6. Challenges in Objective Behavior Study:

Objective behavior study, while providing valuable insights into human and animal behavior, is not without its challenges. One of the primary hurdles in this field is the potential for observer bias. Despite efforts to maintain objectivity, researchers may inadvertently introduce their own biases when interpreting behavioral data. This can lead to discrepancies in the findings and hinder the reliability and validity of the research. Additionally, the complex nature of behavior presents a challenge in itself. Human behavior, in particular, is influenced by a multitude of factors including social, cultural, and environmental variables, making it difficult to isolate specific causes and effects. Moreover, ethical considerations arise when conducting objective behavior studies, especially when experiments involve manipulating or observing subjects in controlled settings. Ensuring that research practices adhere to ethical guidelines while maintaining scientific rigor adds another layer of complexity. Another challenge lies in the interpretation of non-verbal behavior. While verbal communication can be analyzed through language and content, non-verbal cues such as body language and facial expressions require careful interpretation and understanding. Misinterpretation of these cues can lead to erroneous conclusions about an individual's motivations or emotional state. Furthermore, the need for interdisciplinary collaboration poses a challenge in objective behavior study. Given the multifaceted nature of behavior, integrating insights from psychology, sociology, neuroscience, and other disciplines is essential for a comprehensive understanding. However, coordinating across disciplines with differing methodologies and terminologies demands concerted effort and effective communication. Lastly, technological advancements, while beneficial, also present challenges in objective behavior study. Rapid developments in technology necessitate continual adaptation and learning to utilize new tools effectively, while ensuring that these innovations do not overshadow the fundamental principles of objective behavior analysis. Overcoming these challenges requires ongoing vigilance, open dialogue, and a commitment to refining methodologies in the pursuit of accurate and meaningful insights into human and animal behavior.

7. The Integration of Objectivity in Modern Psychology:

Embracing objectivity allows for the adoption of systematic observation and experimentation, steering clear of subjective biases that may cloud interpretations of human behavior. As we look forward to the future of psychology, it is imperative to recognize the paramount importance of integrating objective methods into the field. This entails the incorporation of rigorous measurement techniques, utilization of advanced technological tools, and adherence to established principles of reliability and validity. By doing so, researchers can strive towards ensuring the credibility and robustness of their findings. Furthermore, the push towards integrating objectivity fosters a greater degree of transparency and replicability, essential aspects for the advancement of scientific knowledge. It also serves as a means to bridge theoretical models with practical applications, facilitating a more comprehensive understanding of human behavior.

The discourse on integrating objectivity should not undermine the richness of qualitative research in psychology. As we seek to converge towards objectivity, there should be acknowledgment of the nuances and intricacies that subjective experiences bring to the understanding of human behavior. The synergy between objectivity and subjectivity can yield a more holistic comprehension of psychological phenomena, enabling researchers to traverse the complexities inherent in the human mind. Therefore, the integration of objectivity in modern psychology should not operate in silos but rather coexist harmoniously with qualitative approaches, thereby embracing the multilayered nature of human consciousness.

Additionally, the rising challenges facing modern psychology, such as the expansion of digital platforms and global interconnectivity, underscore the need for robust, objective methodologies. The era of big data and artificial intelligence necessitates a heightened emphasis on objective analysis and interpretation, as traditional paradigms may struggle to encapsulate the vast array of human behaviors and interactions permeating digital landscapes. By integrating objectivity, psychologists can aspire to offer valuable insights into the relationships between individuals and the evolving technological milieu.

As we reflect on the journey towards integrating objectivity in modern psychology, it is evident that this transition represents a pivotal juncture in the evolution of psychological research and practice. The pursuit of evidence-based objectivity underpins the commitment to advancing the frontiers of human understanding, contributing to a more nuanced and comprehensive portrayal of the human psyche. It requires a collective dedication from researchers, practitioners, and academicians to transcend traditional boundaries and embrace the transformative potential of objective methodologies. Embracing this transformation, psychology stands poised to revolutionize its approaches and make enduring contributions to the well-being and progress of humanity.

The Stimulus-Response Relationship

1. Fundamental Concepts:

In the field of behavioral psychology, the foundation of the Stimulus-Response (S-R) model is built upon fundamental concepts that shape our understanding of human behavior. At its core, the S-R psychology delves into the relationship between external stimuli and an individual's response, emphasizing the reactive nature of human beings to environmental cues. Central to this framework is the concept of conditioning, wherein associations are formed between specific stimuli and subsequent responses. This classical conditioning process, pioneered by Ivan Pavlov through his renowned experiments with dogs, demonstrated how a neutral stimulus could elicit a response through repeated pairing with a naturally occurring stimulus. Furthermore, the notion of operant conditioning, introduced by B.F. Skinner, explores how behaviors are shaped by their consequences, either through reinforcement or punishment. These foundational principles provide a lens through which we can comprehend and predict human behavior within various contexts. Moreover, the S-R model highlights the significance of antecedent stimuli in triggering behavioral responses, underscoring the role of environmental influences on shaping individual actions. Unveiling the interplay between stimuli and responses, this framework magnifies the pivotal role of environmental factors in molding behavioral patterns.

It also underscores the deterministic perspective of S-R psychology, positing that behavior is predominantly governed by external forces rather than internal mental states. This approach sets the stage for a nuanced analysis of human conduct, delineating the impact of environmental contingencies on shaping behavioral repertoires. By elucidating these fundamental tenets, the S-R psychology not only offers a comprehensive understanding of behavioral phenomena but also lays the groundwork for practical applications in diverse domains such as education, therapy, and organizational management. Understanding how environmental stimuli influence behavioral responses equips practitioners with valuable insights into fostering adaptive behaviors and ameliorating maladaptive patterns.

2. Historical Context and Evolution:

During the early 20th century, behaviorism emerged as a prominent school of thought in psychology, emphasizing the objective study of observable behaviors and the environmental stimuli that elicit specific responses. This departure from introspective methods marked a significant shift in psychological inquiry, sparking a revolution in the understanding of human learning and adaptation. The evolution of S-R psychology also reflects the influence of experimental methodologies, including classical and operant conditioning paradigms, which provided empirical support for the principles governing stimulus-response associations. Furthermore, the historical context encompasses the assimilation of S-R concepts into diverse domains, such as animal research, educational pedagogy, and therapeutic interventions. The utilization of S-R principles in shaping behavioral interventions, educational strategies, and therapeutic modalities underscores the impact of historical developments on contemporary practices. As the field continued to evolve, the application of S-R principles expanded beyond individual behavior to encompass societal phenomena, organizational dynamics, and cultural influences. This broadening scope further propelled the historical evolution of S-R psychology, extending its relevance to multifaceted aspects of human experience and interaction. Additionally, the historical context sheds light on the transformative impact of interdisciplinary collaborations, as the integration of S-R principles with advancements in neuroscientific research and computational modeling has facilitated a more nuanced understanding of the complex mechanisms underlying behavior.

3. Key Figures:

The development of Stimulus-Response (S-R) theory is intertwined with the pioneering work of a number of key psychologists who shaped the way we understand behavioral responses to external stimuli. One such luminary figure is Edward Thorndike, whose groundbreaking research on animal learning laid the foundation for S-R theory. Through his seminal work with puzzle boxes and the formulation of the Law of Effect, Thorndike demonstrated how behaviors are influenced by the consequences they produce.

Ivan Pavlov, another fundamental figure, revolutionized the understanding of S-R relationships through his research on classical conditioning. His experiments involving the salivary reflex in dogs not only provided empirical evidence for the association between stimuli and responses but also offered valuable insights into the process of associative learning. Pavlov's work has had a lasting impact on our comprehension of conditioned reflexes and their role in shaping behavior.

B.F. Skinner, the father of radical behaviorism, further enriched the landscape of S-R theory. By introducing the concept of reinforcement schedules and operant chambers, Skinner elucidated the principles governing voluntary responses to environmental stimuli. His experiments with pigeons and rats exemplified the influence of consequences on behavioral modification, contributing to the comprehensive understanding of S-R dynamics.

Mary Cover Jones, often revered as the 'mother of behavior therapy,' made remarkable contributions to the practical application of S-R principles in therapeutic settings. Her pioneering work in desensitization techniques for managing phobias showcased the transformative potential of applying S-R theory to real-world behavioral interventions. Jones's innovative approaches laid the groundwork for subsequent advancements in behavior therapy, underscoring the relevance of S-R theory in clinical practice.

In addition to these pivotal figures, the collaborative efforts of numerous researchers and scholars have collectively advanced the S-R framework. The collective contributions of these key figures have not only shaped the theoretical underpinnings of S-R theory but have also catalyzed its translation into diverse domains, encompassing education, clinical psychology, and behavioral interventions. The influence of these trailblazing individuals underscores the interdisciplinary significance of S-R theory, positioning it as a cornerstone in the study of human and animal behavior.

4. Practical Applications and Examples:

In the sphere of practical applications, the stimulus-response mechanism holds significant relevance across various fields. From education to marketing, and from healthcare to criminal justice, the understanding of S-R theory has led to profound implications in shaping human behavior and decision-making processes. One prominent application can be observed in the domain of education, where educators have utilized S-R principles to design effective learning environments and teaching strategies. For instance, the concept of positive reinforcement, an integral component of S-R theory, has been widely employed to encourage desired behavior among students, thereby enhancing the overall learning experience. Similarly, in the field of marketing, the S-R paradigm has been instrumental in devising persuasive advertising techniques and consumer behavior analysis. By comprehending how stimuli evoke certain responses in individuals, marketers can tailor their campaigns to elicit desired reactions and attitudes towards products or services. Furthermore, within the healthcare sector, S-R theory has been leveraged to address behavioral issues and facilitate positive changes in patient habits. Health professionals often utilize conditioning methods to promote healthier lifestyles or to manage various psychological disorders. In the context of criminal justice, the application of S-R theory extends to the rehabilitation and reintegration of offenders into society. By employing behavior modification techniques grounded in S-R principles, authorities aim to reduce recidivism rates and foster constructive behavioral patterns among ex-convicts. These real-world applications not only exemplify the practical utility of S-R theory but also underscore its profound impact on diverse facets of human interaction and societal development. For instance, consider the applications of S-R theory in addressing phobias and anxiety disorders through exposure therapy, effectively utilizing the principles of extinction and systematic desensitization. Similarly, in promoting pro-social behaviors and communal harmony, the application of operant conditioning reinforces altruistic actions and fosters a sense of civic responsibility. Moreover, the field of sports psychology has embraced S-R theory to enhance athletic performance, employing reinforcement and motivation techniques to optimize training regimens and mental conditioning.

5. Comparison with Cognitive Approaches:

In understanding the role of the stimulus-response model within behavioral psychology, it is imperative to conduct a comparative analysis with cognitive approaches. Cognitive psychology emphasizes the internal mental processes involved in behavior, contrasting with the external focus of S-R theory. One fundamental distinction lies in their respective definitions of behavior - while S-R theory centers on observable actions elicited by external stimuli, cognitive psychology delves into the thought processes and mental representations that underpin behavior. This shift in perspective has led to significant implications for our understanding of human behavior and the development of therapeutic interventions.

Particularly noteworthy is the examination of learning and memory within both frameworks. While the S-R model principally concerns itself with associative learning and the modification of behavior through reinforcement and punishment, cognitive psychology has shed light on the complexities of information processing, encoding, storage, and retrieval mechanisms. The interplay between these cognitive processes and behavioral responses has broadened our comprehension of how individuals acquire, retain, and utilize knowledge.

The contrast between S-R theory and cognitive approaches extends to their treatment of motivation and emotion. While the former often views motivation as an external force driving behavior, the latter emphasizes the intrinsic motivation stemming from cognitive evaluations and goal-setting processes. Similarly, cognitive psychology offers nuanced insights into emotional regulation and appraisal, elucidating the interconnections between cognition and affective experiences.

Another crucial point of comparison lies in their respective applications within real-world contexts. While S-R theory has contributed greatly to understanding certain forms of learning, particularly in the domain of conditioning and behavioral modification, cognitive approaches have proven instrumental in fields such as education, clinical psychology, and human-computer interaction. The incorporation of cognitive principles has enriched educational strategies, therapeutic interventions, and the design of user-friendly technological interfaces.

6. Criticisms and Limitations of the Stimulus-Response Model:

The S-R model, while foundational in behavioral psychology, has faced its share of criticisms and limitations. One notable critique revolves around its oversimplified view of human behavior. Critics argue that reducing complex behaviors to simple S-R associations overlooks the intricacies of cognitive processes, emotional states, and individual differences. This reductionist perspective undermines the richness of human experience and neglects the influence of internal mental representations, beliefs, and intentions on behavior.

Additionally, the S-R model has been challenged for its lack of explanatory power in certain contexts. Some scholars point out instances where observed behaviors deviate from predicted responses based on environmental stimuli, suggesting a need for a more comprehensive framework to account for these discrepancies. Furthermore, the rigid nature of the S-R model fails to accommodate the dynamic nature of human behavior, which is influenced by continuous interactions between individuals and their environment.

Another significant limitation lies in the inability of the S-R model to fully address the complexities of associative learning. While it effectively explains basic conditioning phenomena, such as classical and operant conditioning, critics argue that it falls short in elucidating higher-order cognitive functions, such as reasoning, problem-solving, and language acquisition. The emphasis on observable behaviors at the expense of internal cognitive processes limits the model's applicability to a broader range of human behaviors.

Critics also raise concerns about the S-R model's deterministic outlook, which implies that behavior is entirely determined by external stimuli, disregarding individual agency and autonomy. This deterministic view fails to acknowledge the role of personal choice, self-regulation, and volitional control in shaping behavior. Moreover, the model's narrow focus on overt behaviors neglects the internal experiences and subjective interpretations that often drive human action.

Despite these criticisms and limitations, it is important to recognize the historical significance and foundational contributions of the S-R model to the field of behavioral psychology. While acknowledging its constraints, contemporary scholars continue to engage with the model, seeking to integrate it with modern insights from cognitive psychology, neuroscience, and other disciplines to develop a more comprehensive understanding of human behavior.

7. Integration with Contemporary Behavioral Science:

As behaviorism continues to evolve, researchers are exploring how the fundamental principles of S-R theory align with, or diverge from, the findings of cognitive psychology, neurobiology, and other interdisciplinary fields. The bridging of these disparate disciplines is vital for understanding complex human behavior and formulating effective therapeutic interventions.

One significant area of integration lies in the domain of neuroscientific investigations. With the advancement of technologies such as functional magnetic resonance imaging (fMRI) and electroencephalography (EEG), researchers have gained unprecedented insights into the neural underpinnings of behavioral responses. By elucidating the neural correlates of conditioned stimuli and subsequent behavioral reactions, scientists are better placed to validate and refine the S-R model within the context of neural functioning and connectivity. Moreover, this integration has paved the way for novel therapeutic strategies, including neurofeedback training and targeted neuromodulation techniques, that capitalize on the foundational tenets of the S-R model while leveraging neuroscientific knowledge to address maladaptive behaviors and emotional dysregulation.

Contemporary behavioral science has seen a proliferation of research exploring the role of cognition in shaping and moderating stimulus-response associations. While classically rooted in the observable manifestations of behavior, contemporary iterations of behavioral science have increasingly delved into the interplay between cognitive processes and learned behavioral responses. This expanded perspective, often termed cognitive-behavioral integration, acknowledges the symbiotic relationship between perceptual, cognitive, and affective processes in influencing an individual's response to environmental stimuli. By embedding cognitive constructs such as attention, memory, and decision-making within the traditional S-R framework, researchers are striving to construct a more comprehensive model of behavior that accommodates the nuanced interdependence of cognitive and behavioral phenomena.

The integration of the S-R model with contemporary behavioral science extends to its application in addressing clinical conditions and fostering psychological well-being. Cognitive-behavioral therapies (CBT), which draw heavily from both cognitive and behavioral principles, exemplify the marriage of S-R theory with contemporary therapeutic modalities. By amalgamating proven S-R principles with cognitive restructuring techniques and mindfulness-based interventions, CBT has emerged as a cornerstone of evidence-based psychotherapeutic approaches across diverse clinical presentations, ranging from anxiety disorders and mood disturbances to addiction and personality disorders. The continued refinement and empirical validation of such integrative frameworks underscore the relevance and adaptability of the S-R model in the modern landscape of behavioral science and clinical psychology.

Conditioning - Pavlov's Influence and Watson's Adaptation

1. Pavlov's Pioneering Work:

Ivan Petrovich Pavlov, a Russian physiologist who was born in Ryazan in 1849, made crucial contributions to the field of psychology with his work in classical conditioning. His experiments on the digestive processes of dogs led him to the discovery of what he termed 'psychic reflexes,' now known as classical conditioning. Through meticulous experimentation, Pavlov demonstrated that an unconditioned stimulus, such as food, could evoke an unconditioned response, like salivation, in dogs.

Pavlov's research involved the presentation of neutral stimuli, such as a bell, alongside the unconditioned stimulus. Over time, the dogs began to associate the neutral stimulus with the arrival of food, leading to the development of a conditioned response—the salivation excited by the bell alone. This fundamental concept of learning through association laid the groundwork for the theory of classical conditioning.

Pavlov's meticulous attention to detail and relentless pursuit of scientific rigor set a standard for experimental psychology. His innovative approach revealed the adaptive nature of behavior and cognition, sparking a paradigm shift in psychological thought. Moreover, his findings provided a framework for understanding how environmental cues can shape behavior and emotional responses in both humans and animals.

The impact of Pavlov's work extended beyond the sphere of psychology, influencing various fields such as education, advertising, and therapy. The principles of classical conditioning unearthed by Pavlov continue to be applied in diverse settings, serving as a foundation for behavioral modification techniques and therapeutic interventions.

Pavlov's pioneering work not only revolutionized the study of psychology but also emphasized the interconnectedness of physiological and psychological processes. His legacy endures as a testament to the power of empirical research and the influence of foundational discoveries on the evolution of scientific knowledge.

2. Key Experiments and Discoveries:

As previously stated, one of the most notable experiments that strengthened the foundation of classical conditioning was conducted by Watson and Rayner in 1920, famously known as the Little Albert experiment. This study involved conditioning a young child, known as Little Albert, to fear a previously neutral stimulus, a white rat, by pairing it with a loud, startling noise. The demonstration of fear transfer to other similar objects signified the generalization of conditioned responses, a pivotal aspect in the development of behaviorist theories. Furthermore, the work of E. L. Thorndike on the law of effect, which elucidates the concept of instrumental conditioning and operant behavior, added a new dimension to the understanding of learning processes. His puzzle box experiments with cats established the framework for operant conditioning, emphasizing the role of consequences in shaping voluntary behaviors. Additionally, the studies on taste aversion by John Garcia and Robert Koelling in the 1960s introduced the notion of biological preparedness, demonstrating that organisms are evolutionarily predisposed to associate certain stimuli with negative outcomes. This finding challenged the traditional view of all stimuli being equally associable and contributed to the refinement of conditioning paradigms. The collective insights gained from these seminal experiments not only expanded the theoretical underpinnings of behaviorism but also paved the way for further exploration into the complexities of human and animal learning. Such contributions remain integral in contemporary psychology, serving as touchstones for ongoing research and applications in fields such as education, therapy, and behavioral modification.

3. Transition from Pavlov to Watson:

The transition from Pavlov's groundbreaking work to John B. Watson's paradigm heralded a significant theoretical shift in the field of behavioral psychology. Building on Pavlov's experiments, which centered on the principles of classical conditioning involving involuntary responses to stimuli, Watson introduced a bold departure from introspective, subjective models of understanding behavior to an objective, observable, and quantifiable approach. This shift was rooted in Watson's ambition to bring scientific rigor and empirical evidence to the study of human behavior. By emphasizing the external factors that shape behavior over internal mental processes, Watson's behavioral paradigm laid the foundation for modern behaviorism.

Central to this transition was the rejection of unobservable mental events as valid units of analysis in psychology, a stance sharply contrasting with Pavlov's attention to the role of the mind in conditioning. Watson's radical behaviorist perspective, as articulated in his 1913 paper 'Psychology as the Behaviorist Views

It,' explicitly dismissed the study of consciousness and inner experiences, asserting that behavior should be studied in terms of observable actions and environmental stimuli. This theoretical shift challenged traditional psychological paradigms, marking a critical juncture in the evolution of psychological science.

As Watson aimed to establish behaviorism as a rigorous, scientific discipline, he advocated for a focus on overt behavior that could be measured and predicted with precision. His approach emphasized the importance of environmental influences, particularly the impact of conditioning and learning on shaping individual behaviors. Moreover, Watson's emphasis on the role of nurture over nature represented a departure from previous models that prioritized inherent biological factors in determining behavior. This shift redefined the very essence of psychology, giving rise to a pragmatic, experimental approach that underlined the significance of environmental determinants in molding human conduct.

Watson's paradigm not only set the stage for a new era in psychological research but also paved the way for practical applications of behavioral principles in various contexts, including education, advertising, and therapy. This shift engendered an era of experimentation and innovation in behavior modification, highlighting the far-reaching implications of conditioning principles. The seamless transition from Pavlov's foundational work to Watson's radical behaviorism represents a transformative epoch in the history of psychology, precipitating a revolutionary realignment in the study of human behavior.

4. John B. Watson's Behavioral Paradigm:

In establishing a paradigm shift from the introspective methods of the time, Watson emphasized the importance of observable behaviors and external influences on human development and behavior. By focusing on measurable actions rather than abstract mental processes, Watson's work laid the foundation for modern behavioral psychology and its practical applications.

Watson's behavioral paradigm revolved around the concept of environmental determinism, asserting that an individual's behavior is predominantly shaped by their experiences and interactions within their environment. Rejecting the notion of inherited or innate traits as significant determinants of behavior, Watson argued that behaviors are learned through conditioning and environmental influences. This perspective significantly impacted the field of psychology, shifting the focus towards the analysis of external stimuli and responses.

Central to Watson's paradigm was the belief that behavior could be understood and predicted through rigorous experimentation and study. His famous 'Little Albert' experiment, where he demonstrated the principles of classical conditioning by eliciting fear in a young child, exemplified his empirical approach. Emphasizing the influence of associative learning and stimulus-response relationships, Watson's experimental methodologies provided valuable insights into the mechanisms underlying human behavior.

Watson's paradigm played a pivotal role in challenging Freudian psychoanalytic theories prevalent at the time. By highlighting the role of the environment in shaping behavior, Watson's work called into question the significance of unconscious drives and emphasized the impact of external factors on an individual's development and actions. This shift prompted a reevaluation of psychological research methods and theoretical frameworks, paving the way for a new era in behavioral psychology.

Overall, John B. Watson's behavioral paradigm not only revolutionized the study of human behavior but also contributed to the establishment of behaviorism as a dominant psychological perspective. His emphasis on empirical observation, environmental determinism, and experimental methodologies continues to shape contemporary psychological practices and remains an enduring legacy in the field of psychology.

5. Watson's Experimental Methodologies and Findings:

In his pursuit of establishing behaviorism as a distinct scientific discipline, Watson conducted a series of experiments. Central to his methodology was the meticulous observation and documentation of animal behavior in controlled laboratory settings. By focusing extensively on observable behaviors, Watson sought to eliminate subjective interpretations and delve into the empirical study of conditioned responses. Through the careful manipulation of stimuli and environmental cues, Watson devised experiments that aimed to elucidate the principles of classical conditioning in real-time scenarios. One of the most renowned experiments was the 'Little Albert' study, where an infant was presented with various stimuli to examine the acquisition of fear responses through conditioning. Watson's findings from this study provided profound insights into the process of fear conditioning and the potential for emotional responses to be shaped through environmental influences. Furthermore, his pioneering work laid the groundwork for understanding the transferability of conditioned responses across different stimuli and contexts. Watson's rigorous approach to experimentation revolutionized the scientific study of behavior and paved the way for systematic investigations into the principles of learning and conditioning. His dedication to methodological precision and empirical verification remains a cornerstone of modern behavioral research, serving as a testament to the impact of his experimental methodologies. The culmination of Watson's research efforts yielded invaluable findings that continue to shape our understanding of behavioral conditioning and its implications for human and animal behavior. His relentless pursuit of scientific rigor and objective inquiry established a paradigm shift within psychology, propelling behaviorism to the forefront of psychological discourse and reshaping the contours of psychological inquiry.

6. Practical Applications of Pavlovian Principles by Watson:

The founder of behaviorism was not only focused on developing theoretical frameworks but also on applying these principles to practical settings. Watson's implementation of Pavlovian principles revolutionized various fields, ranging from child psychology to advertising.

One notable application was in the field of child development. Watson's experiments with the concept of 'behavioral conditioning' significantly impacted the understanding of child-rearing practices. He emphasized the importance of environmental stimuli and responses in shaping a child's behavior. This led to a more systematic approach to parenting and education, advocating for the use of positive reinforcement to mold desirable behaviors in children.

Watson's work laid the foundation for the application of behavioral principles in clinical psychology. By drawing from Pavlov's classical conditioning, Watson introduced the concept of behavior therapy. This therapeutic approach focused on modifying maladaptive behaviors through conditioning techniques. It opened new avenues for treating various psychological disorders, paving the way for modern behavior modification therapies.

Another area where Watson's practical applications were profound is in the domain of advertising and marketing. Leveraging the principles of classical conditioning, Watson demonstrated how consumer behavior could be influenced through strategic product placement and associative messaging. His insights profoundly shaped the field of advertising, leading to the development of sophisticated marketing strategies based on behavioral conditioning.

In addition to these domains, Watson's practical applications extended to the spheres of animal training and organizational behavior. His research contributed to the refinement of animal training methods, emphasizing the role of reinforcement in shaping animal behavior. Moreover, his insights were instrumental in understanding and managing employee behaviors within organizations, thereby influencing the field of organizational psychology.

Overall, Watson's practical applications of Pavlovian principles transcended theoretical boundaries and permeated various aspects of human life. Through his pioneering work, he not only advanced the field of behaviorism but also laid the groundwork for utilizing conditioning principles in diverse practical contexts, leaving a lasting impact on psychology, education, marketing, and beyond.

7. Comparison of Pavlov and Watson's Theories:

Pavlov's classical conditioning and Watson's behaviorist theories represent two influential pillars in the early development of behavioral psychology. While both approaches share common ground in their focus on learned behaviors, there are fundamental divergences in their theoretical underpinnings. Pavlov's work centered on the fundamental association between a neutral stimulus and an unconditioned response, showcasing the process of learning through repeated pairings. In contrast, Watson extended this concept by emphasizing the influence of environmental factors in shaping behavior, disregarding the role of internal mental processes. This dichotomy serves as a springboard for a comprehensive comparative analysis. One key differentiator lies in their respective views on the role of consciousness. Pavlov acknowledged the presence of subjective experiences, acknowledging the influence of cognition on conditioning, albeit in a limited capacity. Conversely, Watson staunchly rejected the consideration of consciousness in his study of behavior, advocating for a purist focus on observable stimuli and responses. Another distinguishing factor is their experimental methodologies; while Pavlov utilized animal subjects to explore salivary reflexes, Watson transitioned to studying human infants to investigate emotional responses, highlighting the expanded scope of behaviorism. Additionally, the notion of generalization and discrimination plays out differently in their theories, with Pavlov's emphasis on the stimulus's specificities contrasting with Watson's broader application of learned behaviors across contexts. Furthermore, the implications of their theories on practical applications differ, with Pavlov's work forming the basis for therapies like systematic desensitization, and Watson laying the groundwork for the influential field of behavior modification. Unveiling the strengths and limitations of each approach fosters a nuanced understanding of their impact on modern psychological paradigms. Acknowledging Pavlov's emphasis on biological underpinnings and Watson's environmental determinism necessitates an examination that draws from neuroscientific, cognitive, and sociocultural perspectives.

8. Critiques and Limitations of Early Conditioning Models:

Early conditioning models, particularly Pavlovian and behaviorist theories, have significantly contributed to our understanding of conditioned responses and behavior modification. However, these theories are not without their critiques and limitations, which warrant careful examination. One key critique revolves around the reductionist nature of early conditioning models. Critics argue that these theories oversimplify complex human behavior by focusing solely on observable stimuli and responses, neglecting the influence of internal cognitive processes and emotions. Additionally, the deterministic perspective of early conditioning models has been a subject of scrutiny. Critics argue that these models portray individuals as mere products of their environment, disregarding individual agency and free will. This overlooks the interplay between biological, psychological, and environmental factors in shaping behavior. Furthermore, the ethical implications of applying conditioning techniques in human subjects have sparked ethical concerns. The potential for manipulation and coercion in using conditioning methods to modify behaviors raises questions about autonomy and consent. Another limitation pertains to the generalizability of findings from animal studies to human behavior. While early conditioning research heavily relied on animal experimentation, the applicability of these findings to human behavior may be limited, given the inherent differences between species. Moreover, the failure to consider the role of individual differences and diversity in responding to conditioning techniques poses a significant limitation. Variation in personalities, cultural backgrounds, and subjective experiences may influence the effectiveness of conditioning interventions. Lastly, the inability of early conditioning models to account for spontaneous recovery and other phenomena challenges their comprehensive explanatory power. Despite these criticisms, it is imperative to acknowledge the foundational contributions of Pavlov and Watson in paving the way for the development of modern behavioral psychology.

9. Evolution from Classical to Behaviorist Conditioning:

The journey through the critiques and limitations of early conditioning models has revealed a significant evolution from classical to behaviorist conditioning. The classical model provided foundational insights into the mechanisms of associative learning. However, as the discipline progressed, it became evident that a more comprehensive understanding of human behavior necessitated a paradigm shift. This shift culminated in the emergence of behaviorist conditioning.

The evolution from classical to behaviorist conditioning signifies a fundamental departure from the passive nature of classical conditioning to the active, environmental determinism espoused by behaviorism. The foundational premises of behaviorist conditioning challenge traditional assumptions about the role of consciousness and subjective experience in shaping behavior. Instead, emphasis is placed on observable behaviors and the environmental factors that shape and maintain them.

Behaviorist conditioning engenders a practical focus on the application of psychological principles to real-world phenomena. By eschewing the study of internal mental processes, behaviorism places a premium on empirical observation and verifiable experimentation. This ethos has had far-reaching implications across various domains, including education, clinical psychology, and organizational behavior.

The evolution to behaviorist conditioning has prompted an interdisciplinary approach to understanding human behavior. It has fostered collaboration between psychology and other disciplines such as neuroscience, sociology, and computer science, leading to a more holistic comprehension of individual and collective actions.

Emotions as Conditioned Responses

1. Principles of Classical Conditioning in Emotional Response:

Classical conditioning serves as a fundamental framework for understanding the link between environmental stimuli and emotional responses. At its core, classical conditioning involves the association between a neutral stimulus and an unconditioned stimulus to evoke a conditioned response. The process unfolds through repeated pairings of these stimuli, leading to the transformation of the neutral stimulus into a conditioned stimulus that elicits the same response as the unconditioned stimulus.

Emotions, being complex psycho-physiological states, are deeply intertwined with classical conditioning. Through this mechanism, individuals develop emotional associations with specific stimuli, contributing to the formation of behavioral dispositions and affective responses. Understanding the principles of classical conditioning in emotional response is pivotal in comprehending various psychological phenomena, including phobias, anxieties, and emotional disorders.

Research has demonstrated the role of extinction and spontaneous recovery in classical conditioning, shedding light on how emotional responses can be modulated and reactivated over time. The process of extinction involves presenting the conditioned stimulus without the unconditioned stimulus, gradually leading to a reduction in the conditioned response. In contrast, spontaneous recovery refers to the re-emergence of the conditioned response after a period of apparent extinction, emphasizing the nature of emotional conditioning. Examining these phenomena unveils the nuanced dynamics of emotional responses within the framework of classical conditioning.

Additionally, the concept of stimulus generalization and discrimination offers valuable insights into the broadening or narrowing of emotional responses to stimuli resembling or differing from the conditioned stimulus. This characterization underscores the interplay between environmental cues and emotional reactions, elucidating the adaptive nature of emotional conditioning. Furthermore, the concept of higher-order conditioning, wherein a neutral stimulus becomes a conditioned stimulus through association with an existing conditioned stimulus, expands the scope of emotional conditioning to encompass complex cognitive processes.

2. Watson's Experiments - Case Study of Little Albert:

Watson's case study on Little Albert is renowned in the field of psychology aimed to demonstrate how a phobia or emotional response could be conditioned in a young child. The study involved an 11-month-old infant, referred to as 'Albert', who was exposed to various stimuli to investigate the process of fear acquisition and emotional conditioning. Initially, the infant showed no fear responses to a white rat, rabbit, dog, or various other objects. However, through a series of paired associations between these items and loud, startling noises, Watson and his collaborator Rosalie Rayner successfully induced fear and avoidance reactions in the child. The significant outcome of this study was the establishment of a conditioned emotional response in Little Albert, which extended to similar stimuli not originally feared. The unethical nature of the experiment has led to debates regarding research ethics and the treatment of participants in psychological studies. The impact of Watson's experiment on the understanding of fear and emotional conditioning extends beyond the original study, influencing subsequent research and theoretical development in behavioral psychology, particularly in the spheres of phobias, anxiety disorders, and emotional learning. Despite ethical concerns, the Little Albert study stands as a pivotal example of how environmental stimuli can shape emotional responses, providing valuable insights into the mechanisms of fear acquisition and the potential applications in behavioral therapy and interventions.

3. Observable Outcomes - Conditioning Fear and Other Emotions:

The conditioned emotional response observed in Little Albert exemplified the potential for associative learning mechanisms to deeply influence human behavior and emotional reactions. When a previously neutral stimulus (in this case, the white rat) became associated with a loud, startling noise, Little Albert's emotional response - initially absent - transformed into fear and distress. This experiment demonstrated how emotional responses could be conditioned through associative learning, leading to broader implications for the understanding of emotions. Furthermore, the examination of observable outcomes extends beyond fear to encompass a spectrum of emotions that can be influenced and conditioned. The applicability of these findings to various emotional experiences highlights the versatility of associative learning mechanisms in shaping human emotional responses. Additionally, the study of observable outcomes delves into the nuanced nature of emotional conditioning, shedding light on the intricacies involved in eliciting and altering emotional responses. By analyzing the observable manifestations of conditioned emotions, researchers gain valuable insights into the underlying processes and effects of emotional conditioning. This comprehensive analysis provides a more profound understanding of the complex interplay between stimuli, emotional responses, and associative learning, thereby enriching the discourse surrounding emotional conditioning and its impact on human psychology. The investigation also considers the ethical implications of conditioning emotions, emphasizing the need for responsible and conscientious research practices in studying such sensitive phenomena. As the study of observable outcomes pertaining to emotional conditioning evolves, ongoing inquiries seek to unravel the workings of associative learning mechanisms and their influence on human emotions.

4. Cross-Examination with Animal Studies:

Research on emotional conditioning extends beyond human subjects to encompass a diverse range of animal studies. These investigations provide valuable insights into the underlying mechanisms of conditioned emotional responses, shedding light on the generalizability and applicability of behavioral principles across different species. Through sophisticated experimental designs and rigorous observational methodologies, researchers have probed the processes by which animals develop and exhibit conditioned emotional behaviors. Classical experiments involving Pavlovian conditioning in animals, such as Ivan Pavlov's groundbreaking work with dogs, served as pioneering demonstrations of associative learning and its relevance to emotional responses. Subsequent studies have expanded this line of inquiry to encompass diverse species, including rodents, birds, and non-human primates. This broad scope of research illuminates the fundamental principles of emotional conditioning while elucidating species-specific variations in behavioral and physiological responses. By closely examining the parallels and deviations in emotional conditioning across species, scientists can delineate the core mechanisms from the idiosyncrasies inherent in each species' adaptive and survival strategies. Additionally, comparative investigations facilitate the identification of evolutionary conserved pathways and potential applications in translational research for human emotional disorders. Ethical considerations underpinning the use of animals in these studies are paramount, prompting ongoing efforts to ensure humane treatment and minimize distress. This involves stringent adherence to institutional and regulatory guidelines, such as those outlined in the principles of the 3Rs - Replacement, Reduction, and Refinement. These guiding principles emphasize the ethical imperative to seek alternatives to animal use, reduce the number of animals involved, and refine experimental procedures to minimize harm and distress. While animal studies yield invaluable contributions to our understanding of emotional conditioning, ethical considerations must continually inform and guide research practices to uphold the welfare of animal subjects. Furthermore, conscientious reflection on the transferability of findings from animal models to human emotional experiences is essential, warranting cautious interpretation of results and reinforcing the need for complementary research methods.

5. Comparisons with Cognitive Theories of Emotion:

Cognitive theories of emotion propose that emotions are the result of cognitive processes, including interpretation and appraisal of a situation, rather than just conditioned responses. These theories emphasize the role of thoughts, beliefs, and interpretations in the experience and expression of emotions. When comparing cognitive theories with emotional conditioning, it's essential to consider the differing perspectives on the origins and nature of emotions.

One key distinction lies in the influence of past experiences. While emotional conditioning focuses on learned associations through repeated pairings of stimuli, cognitive theories highlight the significance of individual interpretation and meaning-making in shaping emotional experiences. According to cognitive theories, how individuals interpret and appraise their environment directly influences their emotional responses. This stands in contrast to the behavioral perspective, which emphasizes the impact of external stimuli on eliciting emotional reactions.

Cognitive theories underline the role of mental representations and schemas in shaping emotional experiences. The concept of cognitive schemas suggests that individuals have pre-existing mental frameworks that guide their understanding and response to situations, contributing to the diversity of emotional reactions across individuals. In contrast, emotional conditioning explains emotional responses as direct products of environmental cues and learned associations, without the same emphasis on internal cognitive processes.

Another crucial point of comparison is the treatment of irrational or maladaptive emotions. Cognitive theories of emotion often focus on identifying and modifying unhelpful thought patterns and beliefs that contribute to negative emotional states. Therapeutic interventions based on cognitive theories, such as cognitive-behavioral therapy (CBT), aim to restructure cognitive processes to alleviate emotional distress. Conversely, emotional conditioning approaches may primarily seek to alter an individual's learned responses to specific stimuli, without necessarily addressing the underlying cognitive mechanisms contributing to their emotional experiences.

Despite these differences, contemporary psychological research acknowledges the potential integration of both cognitive and conditioning perspectives in understanding the complexities of human emotion. Some scholars have proposed models that incorporate elements of both cognitive and behavioral theories, recognizing the interplay between learned associations and cognitive processing in shaping emotional responses. This integrative approach suggests that emotions may result from a combination of learned associations and cognitive appraisals, highlighting the need for comprehensive and holistic frameworks to account for the multifaceted nature of human emotion.

6. Implications for Therapeutic Practices:

The study of emotional conditioning and its implications for therapeutic practices holds significant promise in the field of clinical psychology and psychotherapy. Understanding how emotions are formed and influenced through conditioning processes provides valuable insights into developing effective therapeutic interventions. By acknowledging the role of environmental stimuli and learned responses in shaping emotional experiences, therapists can tailor treatment plans to address maladaptive emotional reactions.

One of the primary implications lies in the application of systematic desensitization and exposure therapies for individuals suffering from phobias, anxiety disorders, and trauma-related conditions. Through the principles of classical conditioning, therapists can gradually expose clients to fear-inducing stimuli in a controlled and supportive environment, leading to the attenuation of conditioned emotional responses. This process enables individuals to relearn adaptive emotional reactions, thereby reducing their distress and enhancing their quality of life.

Emotional conditioning research has paved the way for the development of cognitive-behavioral therapies (CBT) that incorporate techniques aimed at modifying maladaptive cognitive processes and associated emotional responses. By integrating the principles of emotional conditioning with cognitive restructuring, CBT offers a powerful framework for addressing various psychological disorders, including depression, post-traumatic stress disorder, and obsessive-compulsive disorder. Therapists can work collaboratively with clients to identify and challenge dysfunctional thought patterns while simultaneously implementing behavioral interventions to reshape conditioned emotional responses.

The understanding of emotional conditioning also underscores the importance of creating conducive environments within therapeutic settings. By recognizing the impact of environmental cues on emotional experiences, therapists can create tailored therapeutic contexts that facilitate positive emotional associations and help in preventing the reinforcement of maladaptive emotional reactions. This approach encompasses the utilization of pleasant and calming stimuli to counteract negative emotional conditioning, thereby fostering an atmosphere conducive to emotional healing and growth.

Additionally, the application of emotional conditioning principles extends to the sphere of addiction treatment and relapse prevention. By identifying and addressing conditioned cues and triggers associated with substance use and addictive behaviors, therapists can design comprehensive interventions that target both the cognitive and emotional aspects of addiction. Through the incorporation of cue exposure therapy and the reconditioning of emotional responses to addiction-related cues, individuals undergoing rehabilitation can develop heightened resilience against relapse and gain better control over their emotional reactions.

7. Critical Reflections on Methodology and Findings:

In examining the methodology and findings related to emotional conditioning, it is imperative to engage in critical reflections that illuminate both strengths and limitations of the existing research. One fundamental aspect requiring scrutiny is the methodological approach adopted in studying the phenomenon of emotional conditioning. While traditional experiments have demonstrated the capacity to establish associative learning processes in controlled laboratory settings, questions arise regarding the generalizability of such findings to real-world scenarios. The artificial nature of laboratory conditions may not accurately mirror the complexity of environmental stimuli encountered in everyday life, thereby warranting caution when extrapolating these results to practical contexts. Furthermore, concerns regarding the ethics of inducing emotional responses through conditioning techniques necessitate careful consideration of the implications for participants' well-being and autonomy. This prompts researchers to explore alternative methodologies that prioritize participant welfare while maintaining scientific rigor. Additionally, a critical examination of the findings from emotional conditioning studies is indispensable for refining existing theoretical models. Scrutinizing the empirical evidence aids in discerning the nuances of emotional responses and their associative underpinnings. By scrutinizing the consistency of findings across diverse populations and environmental conditions, researchers can establish a more comprehensive understanding of the universal versus context-specific aspects of emotional conditioning. These reflective processes drive the evolution of theoretical frameworks and contribute to the cultivation of nuanced perspectives that transcend reductionist interpretations of emotions as mere conditioned responses. Moreover, an introspective evaluation of the limitations inherent in experimental design and data interpretation fosters intellectual humility and promotes a culture of rigorous inquiry within the field. By acknowledging the boundary conditions and potential confounds affecting experimental outcomes, researchers lay the groundwork for future studies that address these challenges to refine our comprehension of emotional conditioning phenomena. Ultimately, fostering a reflexive attitude toward methodological choices and empirical findings is integral to upholding the integrity and relevance of research in emotional conditioning, propelling the discipline toward greater sophistication and applicability.

Principles of Generalization, Discrimination, and Extinction

1. Generalization in Behavioral Responses:

Generalization in behavioral responses refers to the phenomenon where an organism demonstrates a conditioned response to stimuli that are similar, but not identical, to the original conditioned stimulus. This process plays a fundamental role in understanding how learned behaviors manifest in various real-world contexts. At its core, generalization allows for adaptive responses to novel stimuli that exhibit resemblance to the original conditioning, promoting flexibility and survival in diverse environments. To illustrate this principle, consider a classic example from the field of psychology: a child who has been conditioned to fear a specific type of dog may also exhibit fear responses to other breeds of dogs or even animals with similar physical characteristics. This occurrence highlights how generalization extends the conditioned response beyond the exact stimulus that was originally paired with an unconditioned response. Understanding the mechanisms and boundaries of generalization holds great significance in both theoretical and practical applications within the sphere of behavioral psychology.

2. Mechanisms of Response Generalization:

Response generalization elucidates the breadth of an organism's learned responses beyond specific stimuli. This phenomenon occurs when an individual exhibits a conditioned response to stimuli that are similar, but not identical, to the original conditioned stimulus. The mechanisms underlying response generalization are multifaceted and have significant implications for both theoretical understanding and practical application. One fundamental mechanism of response generalization involves the perceptual elements of stimuli. When stimuli share common features with the original conditioned stimulus, individuals may generalize their learned response to these similar stimuli. This automatic transfer of response allows for adaptation to new situations, facilitating the application of previously acquired behaviors to novel contexts. Furthermore, response generalization can be shaped by the cognitive processes of abstraction and categorization. Through abstraction, individuals recognize the commonalities among various stimuli and generate generalized responses based on these similarities. Categorization also plays a pivotal role, as individuals classify diverse stimuli into relevant categories and apply learned responses accordingly. Beyond perceptual and cognitive mechanisms, response generalization can be influenced by environmental settings and contextual cues. Situational factors, such as the setting, timing, or social context, can prompt the generalization of learned responses. Additionally, emotional congruence between stimuli can evoke generalization, wherein stimuli eliciting similar emotional reactions can trigger comparable learned responses. The complex interplay of these mechanisms contributes to the comprehensive nature of response generalization and highlights the processes involved in adaptive behavioral responses. Understanding the mechanisms of response generalization is indispensable for designing interventions aimed at promoting adaptive behaviors and mitigating maladaptive responses. It provides valuable insights into the malleability of learned behaviors across varied contexts, offering opportunities for tailored behavior modification strategies. Moreover, this knowledge fosters a deeper comprehension of how individuals traverse their environments, adapt to new challenges, and exhibit flexible behaviors based on past experiences. As such, the exploration of response generalization is essential for advancing the understanding of behavioral conditioning and its far-reaching implications across diverse domains.

3. Discrimination Processes in Conditioning:

Discrimination processes in conditioning refer to the ability of an organism to distinguish between different stimuli and respond selectively based on these distinctions. This critical aspect of conditioning plays a pivotal role in shaping behavior and has been extensively studied within the framework of behavioral psychology. The ability to discriminate between similar stimuli is fundamental for adaptive behaviors and encompasses both classical and operant conditioning paradigms.

In classical conditioning, discrimination occurs when an organism learns to respond to one specific stimulus while inhibiting the same response to other similar stimuli. Experimental evidence has demonstrated how animals and humans can be trained to differentiate between various stimuli through systematic reinforcement and extinction procedures. Such studies have highlighted the precision with which organisms can learn to discern subtle variations in their environment and adjust their behavioral responses accordingly.

Discrimination processes extend to operant conditioning, where organisms learn to differentiate between reinforcements or punishments based on specific cues or contextual factors. The ability to discriminate between the consequences of different actions is integral to understanding the contingencies that govern behavioral outcomes. Through reinforcement schedules and discriminated operant tasks, researchers have elucidated the nature of discrimination learning and its implications for real-world behavior modification.

The broader implications of discrimination processes can be observed in diverse contexts, ranging from clinical settings to educational interventions. For instance, individuals with phobias may undergo discrimination training to distinguish between safe and fear-inducing stimuli, ultimately mitigating their emotional responses. Similarly, educators employ discrimination training to reinforce desired behaviors in students while extinguishing undesirable responses. Understanding the underlying mechanisms of discrimination allows for targeted interventions that promote adaptive behaviors and alleviate maladaptive patterns.

4. Experimental Evidence of Discrimination:

Experimental evidence of discrimination in conditioning processes has been a focal point of research within behavioral psychology. By investigating the ability of organisms to differentiate between stimuli, researchers have shed light on the intricacies of discriminative learning. One classic experiment by Guttman and Kalish (1956) sought to elucidate the concept of stimulus discrimination in pigeons. The study involved training pigeons to peck at discs of different colors, with reinforcement only provided for pecking at a specific color. Through meticulous shaping procedures, the pigeons learned to discriminate between the reinforced color and other non-reinforced colors, thereby displaying evidence of stimulus discrimination. This seminal study showcased the capability of animals to exhibit selective responses based on discernible stimuli, highlighting the importance of discriminative cues in behavioral conditioning. Furthermore, experiments utilizing operant conditioning paradigms have delineated the role of discriminative stimuli in shaping and maintaining complex behaviors. For instance, in a study conducted by Neuringer (1967), rats were trained to press a lever under specific conditions of light intensity and pattern. The results demonstrated that the rats discriminated distinct environmental cues, exhibiting lever-pressing behavior contingent upon the presence of discriminative stimuli. These findings underscore the relevance of discrimination training in modulating behavioral responses. Additionally, research employing aversive conditioning has elucidated the implications of stimulus discrimination in fear generalization and extinction. Studies on fear conditioning in rodents have revealed that precise discrimination between conditioned and neutral stimuli can lead to more targeted fear responses and facilitate extinction processes. Overall, the wealth of experimental evidence provides compelling support for the critical role of discrimination in conditioning and its profound impact on behavior. Such studies deepen our understanding of how organisms discern and respond to specific environmental cues, offering valuable insights for applications in areas such as animal training, education, and clinical interventions.

5. The Concept and Role of Extinction:

Extinction represents the diminishing or suppression of a previously reinforced behavior. In the context of classical conditioning, extinction occurs when the conditioned stimulus (CS) no longer elicits the conditioned response (CR) because it is no longer paired with the unconditioned stimulus (US). Similarly, in operant conditioning, extinction refers to the reduction in the frequency or strength of a behavior when it is no longer followed by a reinforcing consequence.

Understanding the process of extinction is essential for comprehending the complexities of human and animal behavior. By systematically exploring the conditions under which extinction occurs, researchers have unearthed valuable insights into the underlying mechanisms of learning and memory. This has significant implications for a wide range of fields, including education, clinical psychology, and animal training.

The role of extinction extends beyond its theoretical significance, as it also holds practical relevance in various real-world scenarios. For instance, in therapeutic settings, the deliberate use of extinction procedures can aid in the reduction of maladaptive behaviors such as phobias, anxiety disorders, and substance abuse. Employing carefully designed extinction protocols, therapists can effectively diminish the strength of conditioned responses, ultimately contributing to the alleviation of psychological distress and improvement of overall well-being.

In educational contexts, educators and trainers leverage the principles of extinction to modify undesirable behaviors and reinforce more desirable ones. Through consistent application of extinction techniques, unwanted classroom behaviors or habits can be gradually replaced by more favorable alternatives, fostering a positive and conducive learning environment.

It is important to note that while extinction may result in the suppression of a previously learned behavior, it does not erase the original learning. Instead, it introduces new learning that inhibits the expression of the old behavior. Thus, the intermittent re-emergence of extinguished behaviors, known as spontaneous recovery, underscores the complex nature of extinction processes and highlights the necessity for continued diligence in behavioral interventions.

6. Practical Applications of Extinction Strategies:

Extinction strategies, derived from the principles of behavioral psychology, offer a myriad of practical applications across various domains. In clinical settings, these strategies are utilized to modify maladaptive behaviors, such as addiction, phobias, and compulsions. By systematically removing the reinforcing stimuli associated with these behaviors, extinction aims to diminish their occurrence, thereby fostering adaptive responses. Behavior modification programs for substance abuse, for instance, often incorporate extinction techniques to weaken the association between drug use and environmental triggers, promoting abstinence and long-term recovery.

In educational contexts, extinction strategies play a pivotal role in addressing undesirable behavior patterns among students. By withdrawing reinforcement previously linked to disruptive behaviors, educators strive to eliminate these actions and encourage more positive conduct. This approach not only facilitates a conducive learning environment but also equips students with valuable skills in self-regulation and social interaction.

In organizational management, extinction strategies can be deployed to reshape employee behavior and foster a harmonious workplace culture. By withholding reinforcement for counterproductive actions and emphasizing the desired conduct, leaders can effectively steer organizational dynamics towards enhanced productivity and collaboration. Additionally, proactive implementation of extinction procedures in customer service settings can mitigate undesired customer behaviors and enhance overall service quality.

Extinction strategies also find relevance in animal training and husbandry practices. Through the systematic removal of positive or negative stimuli, trainers aim to eliminate unwanted behaviors and cultivate desired responses in various animals. This is particularly evident in zoological institutions and domestic pet training, where extinction methodologies form the basis of effective behavior management protocols.

Beyond these applications, extinction strategies hold promise in addressing environmentally harmful activities. By inhibiting the reinforcement linked to detrimental environmental practices, societies and governments can curb behaviors that contribute to ecological degradation, ultimately promoting sustainable living and conservation efforts.

Overall, the multifaceted application of extinction strategies underscores their profound impact on human behavior, organizational dynamics, education, and environmental stewardship. Their systematic implementation presents an invaluable tool for fostering positive behavioral change across diverse spheres, serving as a testament to the significance of behavioral psychology in contemporary society.

7. Interrelationships Between the Three Principles:

In understanding the interrelationships between the principles of generalization, discrimination, and extinction, it is crucial to recognize the complex dynamics that govern behavioral responses. While each principle operates distinctly, they are intertwined, influencing and shaping one another in various ways. Generalization, the tendency for a conditioned response to occur in the presence of stimuli similar to the original conditioned stimulus, can also affect the process of discrimination. For instance, if an individual responds to a specific cue, but then demonstrates a similar response to other cues that resemble the original stimulus, it highlights the influence of generalization on discrimination. Similarly, extinction, the reduction in the frequency or strength of a learned response due to the absence of reinforcement, can impact both generalization and discrimination. When extinction is applied to a particular stimulus, it may lead to the weakening of generalization to similar stimuli and aid in refining discriminatory responses. Furthermore, the ability to discriminate between different stimuli can also impede generalization, as individuals learn to differentiate between specific cues and consequently inhibit generalized responses. These intricacies underscore the reciprocal influence and mutual dependence of these principles within the paradigm of behavioral conditioning. This interconnectedness holds significant implications for practical applications, as interventions targeting one principle may inadvertently impact the others. Acknowledging the interplay between these principles is essential for devising comprehensive strategies that effectively modify and shape behavioral patterns.

Rejection of Consciousness in Psychological Study

1. Historical Context and the Role of Introspection:

During the late 19th and early 20th centuries, introspection was a prominent method in psychological research. Stemming from structuralism, introspection involved individuals reflecting on their internal experiences and reporting their conscious thoughts and feelings. However, this approach had several perceived shortcomings that prompted a shift in the field of psychology. Introspection was criticized for its inherently subjective nature, as it relied on self-reporting and individual interpretation of mental processes. It lacked standardization, leading to inconsistent results and making it difficult to replicate findings across different studies. Additionally, introspection faced challenges in capturing unconscious processes and behaviors that were not readily accessible to conscious awareness. This limitation hindered a comprehensive understanding of human cognition and emotion. The reliance on introspection also raised questions about the validity and reliability of the data obtained, casting doubts on the scientific rigor of psychological research. As a result, the historical context highlights the gradual emergence of skepticism towards introspection and paved the way for a more objective and empirical approach to studying behavior and mental processes.

2. Rationale for Dismissing Consciousness as a Study Component:

Consciousness has long been considered a contentious topic in the field of psychology. Early behaviorist theorists, such as Watson and Skinner, played a pivotal role in shaping the rationale for dismissing consciousness as a study component. Their paradigm-shifting work emphasized the need to focus on observable behaviors rather than delving into subjective and introspective aspects of human experience. By redirecting the discipline towards measurable and quantifiable elements, they aimed to establish psychology as a rigorous science. The rationale for dismissing consciousness was rooted in the quest for objectivity and empirical validity. Introspection, a prevailing method at the time, was criticized for its lack of reliability and reproducibility. This led to a growing skepticism towards the significance of subjective experiences in scientific inquiry. Additionally, behaviorists highlighted the inherent ambiguity and imprecision associated with the study of consciousness, which further fueled their stance on prioritizing observable behaviors. They contended that consciousness was elusive, ambiguous, and often resistant to precise definition. As a result, the emphasis shifted towards mechanisms that could be objectively studied and empirically validated. This shift symbolized a departure from traditional approaches and paved the way for the establishment of behaviorism as a dominant force in psychology. The rationale for dismissing consciousness as a study component was underpinned by the desire to elevate psychology to the status of a natural science, characterized by verifiable laws and principles. By shunning the enigmatic nature of consciousness, behaviorists sought to align psychology with the scientific methodologies embraced in fields such as physics and biology. The overarching goal was to foster a discipline grounded in empirical evidence and free from subjective conjecture. Through this lens, the dismissal of consciousness can be perceived as a deliberate step towards positioning psychology as a legitimate and respected scientific endeavor. While controversies abound regarding the exclusion of consciousness from psychological inquiry, it is undeniable that behaviorist thinkers laid the foundation for an empirical and objective approach that has significantly shaped the trajectory of modern psychology.

3. Influence of Early Behaviorist Theorists:

Early behaviorist theorists significantly shaped the landscape of modern psychology, primarily through their emphasis on observable behaviors and the rejection of consciousness as a viable subject of study. One of the foundational events of the movement was the publication of Watson's 1913 paper, 'Psychology as the Behaviorist Views It', where he laid the groundwork for a radical shift in psychological inquiry by promoting the notion that psychology should be redefined as the science of behavior, eschewing mentalistic concepts and focusing on the conditioned relationships between stimuli and responses. This departure from introspective methods, which were prevalent in structuralist psychology at the time, marked a watershed moment in the discipline's history. Behaviorism also drew from the work of Ivan Pavlov, whose research on classical conditioning with dogs provided empirical evidence for the influence of environmental stimuli on behavior. Pavlov's findings further bolstered the argument for prioritizing observable behaviors within scientific study. Beyond these individual contributions, early behaviorist theorists collectively challenged the prevailing paradigms of psychology, instigating profound changes in research methodologies and theoretical frameworks. Their collective influence led to the widespread adoption of experimental methods and rigorous empirical validation, setting the stage for the development of modern psychological science. Moreover, the advocacy for an objective, quantifiable approach to understanding human behavior not only revolutionized academic psychology but also reverberated throughout related disciplines and practical applications.

4. The Shift Towards Observable Behaviors:

In the field of psychology, a notable paradigm shift occurred with the emergence and proliferation of behaviorism. This aforesaid revolution is characterized by a pronounced pivot towards observable behaviors as the focal point of psychological inquiry, marking a departure from the introspective methods dominant in earlier psychological research. Behaviorism sought to establish psychology as an empirical science, emphasizing objectivity and measurability. As such, the focus on observable behaviors aligned seamlessly with behaviorist principles, enabling researchers to investigate and analyze responses that were objectively discernible and quantifiable. This shift was augmented by the development of experimental methodologies that enabled the precise observation and measurement of behavior, thus providing a solid foundation for scientific investigation. With this newfound emphasis on behavior, psychologists were able to apply controlled experimental designs to elucidate the underlying mechanisms governing human and animal conduct. The shift towards observable behaviors also brought about a keen interest in conditioning and learning, as these processes could be readily observed and manipulated within the frameworks established by behaviorist principles. In essence, the pivot towards observable behaviors catalyzed a fundamental transformation in the approach to psychological study, paving the way for a more rigorous and systematic examination of human and animal behavior. Moreover, this shift propelled psychology into the domain of natural sciences, where phenomena could be subjected to empirical scrutiny, leading to the establishment of a robust foundation for the modern discipline of psychology.

5. Subjectivity in Psychological Research:

The reliance on introspection and the interpretation of individuals' inner experiences has often led to subjective biases, making it challenging to achieve objective conclusions. This subjective element introduces variability and hinders the replicability of findings, undermining the credibility of psychological studies. Critics argue that the inherently personal nature of introspection allows for individual differences to influence the reported experiences, impacting the reliability of data. Furthermore, the interpretative nature of subjective reports poses challenges in establishing consistent measurement criteria, leading to potential discrepancies in research outcomes. As such, there is a strong argument to reduce reliance on subjective introspective data in favor of more objective measures. Overemphasis on subjective experiences can also limit the generalizability of findings, as these experiences may not be representative of broader populations. In contrast, objective behavioral observations and physiological measurements offer a more standardized approach, providing quantifiable data that can be analyzed and compared across diverse samples. By shifting the focus from subjective introspection to observable behaviors and measurable physiological responses, psychology can elevate its scientific rigor, enhancing the validity and reliability of its research. Additionally, moving away from subjectivity promotes greater transparency and reproducibility, essential aspects of robust scientific inquiry. The move towards objectivity also aligns with the core principles of behaviorism, emphasizing the study of observable behaviors over internal mental processes. This shift not only addresses the limitations associated with subjectivity but also aligns with the broader scientific community's emphasis on empirical evidence and testable hypotheses. However, it is crucial to recognize that complete dismissal of subjectivity may overlook valuable insights into the human experience. Thus, the critique of subjectivity should be balanced with an appreciation for the nuanced complexities of human cognition and emotion. Integrating both objective and subjective approaches can enrich the field of psychology, offering a comprehensive understanding of human behavior.

6. Consciousness in Contrast to Behavior:

Consciousness, a topic of perennial debate and fascination within the sphere of psychology, presents a unique challenge when attempting to define it in relation to behavior. While behavior pertains to observable actions and reactions, consciousness encapsulates the subjective experiences, thoughts, and awareness possessed by individuals. The contrast between the two concepts lies in the tangibility of behavior versus the intangibility of consciousness. Behavior, being external and measurable, has historically garnered more attention due to its objective nature, allowing for quantitative analysis. On the other hand, consciousness, with its qualia and internal nature, has often been considered immeasurable and elusive, thus leading to its dismissal or neglect in psychological study. Understanding this dichotomy is pivotal in grasping the complexities inherent in the rejection of consciousness as a focal point of psychological research. The dichotomy prompts contemplation on how behaviorism, with its emphasis on quantifiable and observable phenomena, came to overshadow the significance of consciousness in shaping human experience and understanding the human psyche. This historical privileging of behavior over consciousness has left an indelible mark on the trajectory of psychological enquiry and scholarship. It is imperative to recognize that while behavior provides valuable insights into human conduct and responses to stimuli, consciousness offers an internal narrative that underpins and enriches our interpretation of our actions and experiences. Therefore, a reevaluation of the relationship between consciousness and behavior is indispensable for a comprehensive understanding of human psychology. This necessitates a departure from the traditional dichotomy towards a more integrated approach, where both consciousness and behavior are acknowledged as complementary components of the complex tapestry of human psychology. Such an integration holds the promise of unveiling deeper insights into the intricacies of human cognition, emotion, and motivation, ultimately enriching the scope of psychological inquiry and understanding.

7. Experimental Methods and Empirical Validation:

Experimental methods and empirical validation are core components in the rejection of consciousness in psychological study. By focusing on observable behaviors and measurable responses, behaviorism has revolutionized the approach to understanding human psychology. Utilizing rigorous experimental designs, behaviorists have established a framework for scientific inquiry that prioritizes objectivity and quantifiability.

One of the fundamental experimental methods employed is the use of controlled laboratory studies to investigate behavioral responses under specific stimulus conditions. This involves the precise manipulation of environmental variables to elicit desired behaviors and systematically measure their occurrence. Through this method, behaviorists have been able to establish causal relationships between stimuli and responses, providing empirical evidence for their theories.

Behaviorists have extensively utilized operant conditioning experiments to validate their understanding of behavior. These experiments involve the systematic reinforcement or punishment of specific behaviors to shape and modify them over time. The empirical data derived from these experiments has contributed to the establishment of principles such as reinforcement schedules, extinction, and shaping of behaviors, all of which have practical applications in various fields including education, clinical psychology, and organizational behavior management.

In addition to laboratory experiments, behaviorists have also conducted extensive field studies to observe and document naturalistic behaviors in real-world settings. By carefully observing and recording behaviors in their natural environment, behaviorists have been able to glean insights into the influence of environmental factors on behavior while avoiding the biases associated with introspection and subjective interpretation.

The reliance on empirical validation has enabled behaviorism to transcend philosophical debates and become a respected scientific discipline. The emphasis on quantifiable data and replicable experimental outcomes has elevated behaviorism to a position of prominence within psychology, offering tangible contributions to our understanding of human behavior and cognition.

8. Contributions to Science from Bypassing Consciousness:

The bypassing of consciousness in psychological study has yielded significant contributions to the field of science. By focusing on observable behaviors and measurable responses, researchers have been able to apply rigorous experimental methods and empirical validation to their studies. This shift has allowed for the development of objective and replicable findings, enhancing the credibility and reliability of psychological research. As a result, the scientific community has gained valuable insights into various aspects of human behavior and cognition, leading to advancements in numerous subfields of psychology.

One of the key advantages of bypassing consciousness is the ability to conduct controlled experiments and manipulate variables without the influence of subjective introspection. This approach has facilitated the identification of causal relationships between specific stimuli and behavioral responses, enabling researchers to formulate robust theories and models. Furthermore, the emphasis on non-conscious processes has fostered interdisciplinary collaboration, particularly with neuroscientists and cognitive psychologists, leading to a more comprehensive understanding of the underlying mechanisms that drive human behavior.

By excluding reliance on subjective experiences and internal mental states, the study of non-conscious processes has provided practical applications in various domains, including clinical psychology, organizational behavior, and consumer behavior. For instance, the principles derived from non-conscious studies have been instrumental in designing effective behavior modification interventions, improving decision-making processes, and understanding the impact of environmental cues on human behavior.

Additionally, the bypassing of consciousness has contributed to the development of innovative research methodologies and technological advancements. From sophisticated neuroimaging techniques to behavioral experiments in controlled settings, researchers have harnessed the power of non-conscious processes to uncover fundamental principles of human behavior and cognition. This has paved the way for groundbreaking discoveries and theoretical frameworks that continue to shape the landscape of contemporary psychology.

9. Comparison of Conscious vs. Non-Conscious Studies:

Conscious studies, rooted in introspection and subjective self-reporting, have historically dominated psychology, yielding valuable insights into human cognition and behavior. However, concerns regarding objectivity and reliability have led to a paradigm shift toward non-conscious studies, which emphasize observable behaviors and empirical data. Comparative analysis reveals distinct advantages and limitations associated with these divergent approaches. Conscious studies offer in-depth introspective data, illuminating individual experiences and subjective perceptions; conversely, non-conscious studies provide tangible, replicable evidence through controlled experimentation. While conscious studies may unearth nuanced nuances in human consciousness, non-conscious studies offer more universally applicable findings due to their reliance on observable, external phenomena. Critically evaluating both paradigms leads to the recognition that a balanced integration of both conscious and non-conscious methodologies is essential for comprehensive psychological inquiry. Moreover, the progression towards incorporating interdisciplinary methods, including neuroscientific and behavioral analyses, highlights the value of synthesizing diverse approaches to advance psychological understanding.

10. The Long-Term Implications for Psychology:

The shift away from consciousness as a central focus in psychological study has opened up new horizons and possibilities for the field. This strategic redirection has led to significant breakthroughs in understanding human behavior and emotion from an empirical standpoint, as it empowers researchers to delve deeper into observable phenomena that can be reliably measured and tested. By emphasizing the study of overt behaviors and reactions, psychology has been able to establish more concrete and reproducible findings, moving away from the subjective nature of introspection to a more empirical and objective approach. As a result, this shift has had a profound impact on various subfields within psychology, such as clinical psychology, cognitive psychology, and social psychology.

One of the long-term implications of redirecting focus from consciousness is the potential for more effective and evidence-based therapeutic interventions. By prioritizing observable and measurable behaviors, psychologists can develop targeted interventions that are rooted in empirical data, leading to more successful outcomes for individuals seeking mental health support. Additionally, this shift has contributed to the development and refinement of behavioral therapies, which have shown remarkable efficacy in treating a wide range of psychological disorders.

The move towards non-conscious studies has also fueled advancements in the understanding of the influence of environmental factors on behavior. This emphasis has allowed researchers to explore how external stimuli and environmental triggers shape human responses without the interference of conscious processes. The implications of this reach beyond individual therapy and extend to fields such as organizational psychology, where a deeper understanding of behavioral conditioning can inform strategies for promoting positive organizational culture and productivity.

By bypassing the complexities of consciousness, psychology has been able to make significant strides in understanding and managing unconscious biases and prejudices. This has profound implications for social psychology, as it provides a framework for addressing societal issues related to discrimination and inequality. By focusing on observable behaviors and responses, psychology can develop more effective strategies for mitigating the impact of implicit biases in various contexts, fostering inclusivity and equity.

The Impact of Environment over Inherited Traits

1. Introduction to the Nature vs. Nurture Debate:

The nature vs. nurture debate has been a longstanding and contentious issue in the field of psychology, pitting innate biological factors against environmental influences as the primary determinant of human behavior and mental processes. The origins of this debate can be traced back to ancient philosophical traditions, with notable thinkers such as Plato and Aristotle deliberating on the roles of heredity and environment in shaping individual characteristics. This discourse continued through the centuries, gaining new perspectives and dimensions with the advancements in scientific knowledge and empirical research. The debate gained renewed attention in the sphere of modern psychology, where scholars and researchers have sought to unravel the interplay between genetic predispositions and external influences. As the field of behavioral genetics emerged, the debate intensified, with proponents of each viewpoint presenting compelling evidence to substantiate their respective claims. The allure of the nature vs. nurture debate lies in its profound implications for understanding human development, cognition, and behavior, and its relevance extends beyond academic discourse, permeating societal attitudes and public policy considerations. It is important to acknowledge that this debate is not confined to a binary opposition; rather, it encompasses a spectrum of interactions between biological and environmental factors, wherein nuanced discussions are imperative for comprehensive comprehension. In contemporary psychology, interdisciplinary inquiries have shed light on the complex interactional dynamics that underpin human traits and tendencies, advocating for holistic perspectives that embrace the multifaceted contributions of both nature and nurture.

2. Historical Perspectives on Environmental Influences:

Early thinkers such as John Locke and Jean-Jacques Rousseau laid the groundwork for discussions on the role of environmental influences in shaping human development. Locke's empiricist views emphasized the significance of external experiences and sensory stimuli in molding an individual's character, contrasting with Rousseau's romantic beliefs in the inherent purity of human nature before societal corruption. These foundational perspectives set the stage for further exploration into environmental determinants of human behavior. The Industrial Revolution and urbanization during the 18th and 19th centuries also brought attention to the impact of environmental conditions on mental health, prompting reforms in social policies and institutions. Notably, the pioneering work of reformers like Dorothea Dix and Clara Barton highlighted the detrimental effects of poor living conditions on psychological well-being, thus advocating for improved environmental standards. This historical context demonstrates the concern for environmental influences on human behavior across various societal domains. Furthermore, the evolutionary theories of Charles Darwin provided additional impetus for investigating the adaptive significance of environmental interactions. Darwin's theory of natural selection underscored the crucial role of the environment in shaping the survival and reproductive success of species, subsequently influencing the perspectives of early psychologists. The early 20th century witnessed the emergence of behaviorism, wherein scholars like John B. Watson and B.F. Skinner directed attention towards observable behaviors and environmental stimuli, emphasizing the conditioning processes that underlie human actions. This shift in focus from internal mental processes to external environmental inputs marked a pivotal period in the study of environmental influences.

3. Experimental Foundations - Key Studies and Findings:

Through controlled experiments and rigorous data analysis, researchers have endeavored to unravel the relationship between environmental determinants and behavioral outcomes. One seminal study that has significantly contributed to our understanding of environmental impact is the Minnesota Twin Family Study. Initiated in 1989, this longitudinal investigation aimed to assess the relative influence of genetic and environmental factors on various traits and behaviors. By analyzing data from twins raised in different environments, the study underscored the profound impact of environmental determinants on diverse aspects of development, ranging from cognitive abilities to personality traits. These findings highlighted the critical role of environmental factors in shaping individual differences.

The landmark research conducted by Dr. John B. Watson, widely regarded as the father of behaviorism, demonstrated the potent influence of environment through his famous Little Albert experiment. By conditioning a fear response in a young child, Watson showcased how environmental stimuli could significantly impact emotional and behavioral reactions, thereby emphasizing the malleability of human behavior under environmental influences.

Another pivotal study that merits consideration is the Harlow's monkey experiment. This exploration of attachment and socialization in infant rhesus monkeys underscored the significance of social and environmental factors in shaping emotional bonds and developmental outcomes. By understanding the profound impact of nurturing environments on the monkeys' emotional well-being, this study shed light on the critical role of social interactions and environmental enrichment in fostering healthy psychological development.

The adoption studies conducted by developmental psychologists have offered invaluable insights into the interplay between genetic predispositions and environmental factors. Examining the behavioral outcomes of adopted individuals compared to their biological and adoptive parents has elucidated the complex dynamics of heredity and environmental influences, further emphasizing the substantial impact of environmental determinants on individual traits and tendencies.

4. Environmental Determinants of Behavior:

Environment encompasses a wide spectrum of influences, ranging from familial and societal structures to cultural values and physical surroundings. These multifaceted factors mold individuals in profound ways, exerting substantial impact on their behavioral patterns and psychological development. Environmental determinants of behavior are rooted in the concept that external stimuli and experiences play a pivotal role in shaping an individual's personality, emotions, and cognitive processes.

The pervasive influence of the environment becomes particularly evident when observing individuals raised in diverse cultural and socioeconomic contexts. Variations in upbringing, exposure to different value systems, and access to resources profoundly shape the behavioral tendencies and adaptability of individuals. Moreover, environmental determinants extend beyond immediate social surroundings to encompass broader ecological and societal factors. For instance, studies have shown how urban versus rural environments can significantly impact stress levels, coping mechanisms, and overall psychological well-being.

The impact of environmental determinants is linked to the process of socialization, as individuals learn behavioral norms, communication styles, and emotional expressions through their interactions with the environment. This learning process often occurs implicitly, as individuals absorb cues and information from their surroundings, thereby internalizing and exhibiting learned behaviors in various situations.

An essential aspect of investigating environmental determinants of behavior involves exploring the concept of plasticity – the capability of individuals to adapt to diverse environmental conditions. The environmental plasticity hypothesis asserts that human behavior possesses a remarkable degree of adaptability, allowing individuals to adapt to and acclimatize to varying environmental challenges and stimuli. Whether examining the effects of childhood trauma, socio-economic disparities, or cultural assimilation, recognizing the plasticity of human behavior underscores the dynamic nature of the relationship between individual experience and environmental impact.

Notably, contemporary research delves into neuroplasticity, elucidating how the brain responds and adapts to environmental influences through synaptic reorganization and functional changes. Such insights underscore the neurological mechanisms that underpin the profound influence of the environment on behavioral patterns, cognition, and emotional responses. Understanding these mechanisms offers valuable implications for therapeutic interventions, education strategies, and social policy initiatives aimed at fostering optimal environments for psychological well-being and personal growth.

5. The Role of Learning in Shaping Personality:

Personality, as a complex and multifaceted construct, is influenced by various factors, with learning being a pivotal determinant in its development and manifestation. Throughout the lifespan, individuals encounter diverse experiences and stimuli that contribute to the acquisition and adaptation of behaviors deemed characteristic of their personality.

Central to the understanding of personality development is the concept of social learning, which emphasizes the impact of modeling, observation, and reinforcement in shaping individuals' behaviors and characteristics. Bandura's pioneering work on social cognitive theory unveiled the influential role of observational learning, highlighting how individuals emulate and internalize the behaviors and traits they observe in others. Moreover, the principles of operant conditioning elucidate how reinforcements and punishments contribute to the establishment and modification of personality traits, emphasizing the critical role of consequences in shaping individual behavior.

The process of classical conditioning elucidates the learned associations between environmental stimuli and emotional responses, underscoring how past experiences and environmental cues can influence an individual's emotional reactivity and, consequently, personality expression. These learned associations not only shape behavioral responses but also contribute to the development of individual proclivities and aversions, thereby influencing one's overall personality.

Additionally, the role of cognitive processes in personality development cannot be underestimated. The interpretation of experiences, attribution of meaning, and cognitive restructuring all play integral roles in shaping an individual's self-concept and behavioral tendencies. As such, the impact of learning on personality extends beyond mere behavioral manifestations and encompasses cognitive and affective dimensions, illustrating the profound influence of environmental stimuli on the complexity of individual personality.

Ultimately, the relationship between learning and personality underscores the dynamic and adaptive nature of human behavior, affirming the multifaceted influence of environmental factors on the nuanced development of individual traits and dispositions.

6. Interplay Between Environment and Developmental Stages:

The interplay between environment and developmental stages is a subject of profound significance in understanding the complexities of human behavior. Developmental stages encompass crucial periods of growth and change, each presenting unique opportunities for environmental influences to shape individual traits and characteristics. During these formative phases, environmental factors such as family dynamics, socio-economic conditions, cultural upbringing, and educational experiences play pivotal roles in molding an individual's personality, cognition, and emotional regulation.

Early childhood, often regarded as a foundational stage in human development, is particularly susceptible to the influence of the environment. This phase lays the groundwork for crucial cognitive and social skills, with responsiveness to external stimuli shaping neural connections and behavioral patterns. The quality of caregiving, exposure to language, and the presence of nurturing relationships significantly impact the child's ability to form secure attachments and develop emotional resilience.

As children progress through adolescence, the dynamic interplay between biological maturation and environmental factors becomes increasingly apparent. Peer relationships, societal expectations, and access to educational opportunities can profoundly influence self-esteem, identity formation, and moral reasoning. Moreover, varying levels of exposure to stressors, trauma, or supportive resources can markedly impact an adolescent's emotional well-being and adaptive coping strategies.

Transitioning into adulthood, individuals continue to be impacted by environmental forces as they traverse educational pursuits, career choices, and social interactions. The environment, inclusive of workplace culture, community dynamics, and access to resources, shapes vocational aspirations, interpersonal dynamics, and overall life satisfaction. Furthermore, the cumulative effects of environmental exposures over the lifespan contribute to the development of resilience or vulnerability to mental health challenges and emotional regulation.

Understanding the interplay between environment and developmental stages is instrumental in delineating the multifaceted pathways through which individuals acquire behavioral patterns and emotional dispositions. By acknowledging the nuanced influence of the environment at different developmental junctures, researchers and practitioners can cultivate holistic approaches to promoting psychological well-being and adaptive functioning across the lifespan.

7. Genetic Predispositions versus Environmental Conditioning:

The debate surrounding the relative impacts of genetic predispositions and environmental conditioning on human behavior has been a central focus of psychological inquiry. While genetic predispositions are inherent traits that individuals inherit from their parents, environmental conditioning refers to the influence of external factors on an individual's behavioral and emotional development. This dichotomy has sparked numerous studies and debates within the field of psychology, as researchers seek to unravel the interplay between nature and nurture.

Understanding the extent to which genetic factors shape an individual's behavior is a complex endeavor. Genetic predispositions encompass a wide range of characteristics, from physical attributes to temperament and personality traits. It is essential to acknowledge the fundamental role that genetics play in laying the groundwork for an individual's predispositions, which can significantly influence their susceptibility to certain behavioral patterns or psychological conditions.

The concept of environmental conditioning highlights the profound impact of external factors on shaping an individual's behavioral repertoire. Environmental influences, such as upbringing, cultural norms, social interactions, and experiences, all contribute to the development of cognitive and emotional processes. Nurture has been found to play a pivotal role in determining and modifying an individual's behavior, especially during critical periods of development.

The interaction between genetic predispositions and environmental conditioning gives rise to the complexity of human behavior. While genetic factors set the stage for certain propensities, the environment can either exacerbate or mitigate these inclinations through various mechanisms. For instance, a person with a genetic predisposition towards anxiety may exhibit heightened symptoms if exposed to a highly stressful environment, whereas a supportive and nurturing environment might help alleviate the manifestation of anxiety-related behaviors.

Research in behavioral genetics has advanced our understanding of this dynamic by exploring the heritability of specific traits and the extent to which environmental factors modulate them. Longitudinal studies tracking individuals from early childhood into adulthood have provided valuable insights into the lifelong interplay between genetic predispositions and environmental influences. These studies have demonstrated that while genetic factors contribute to the baseline of individual differences, environmental experiences continually shape and mold behavior over time.

8. Longitudinal Studies in Behavioral Adaptation:

Longitudinal studies, often spanning several years or decades, have been fundamental in unraveling the complex interplay between genetics and environmental factors in shaping individual behavior and adaptation. These extensive research endeavors allow for the tracking of individuals over time, providing valuable insights into how traits and behaviors evolve and adapt in response to changing environments.

One notable longitudinal study conducted by a team of researchers at a prominent academic institution followed a cohort of participants from early childhood into adulthood. The study meticulously documented various aspects of the participants' lives, including their familial backgrounds, social interactions, educational experiences, and occupational trajectories. By meticulously collecting and analyzing data at multiple points throughout their lives, the researchers were able to discern patterns of behavioral adaptation and resilience in the face of environmental challenges.

The findings from such longitudinal studies underscore the dynamic nature of human adaptation, highlighting the profound impact of environmental influences on individuals' behavioral trajectories. For instance, the researchers observed that individuals exposed to adverse childhood environments, characterized by neglect or maltreatment, displayed varying degrees of resilience and vulnerabilities as they progressed through adolescence and into adulthood. The intricacies of these long-term effects shed light on the critical importance of early intervention and support mechanisms in fostering positive behavioral outcomes.

Longitudinal studies have contributed to clarifying the relative contributions of genetic predispositions and environmental exposures to behavioral outcomes. By systematically examining the development of specific traits and behaviors over time, researchers have delineated the profound influence of environmental contexts in either amplifying or mitigating genetic propensities. This nuanced understanding has significant implications for devising targeted interventions and strategies to promote adaptive behaviors and mitigate the potential detrimental impacts of adverse environments.

Additionally, longitudinal studies have unveiled key developmental milestones and sensitive periods during which environmental inputs exert maximal influence on behavioral adaptation. Understanding these critical windows of susceptibility informs efforts to implement timely and tailored interventions that capitalize on individuals' receptivity to positive environmental stimuli.

In conclusion, through meticulous observation and analysis, these studies offer unparalleled depth in understanding the complexities of genetic-environment interaction and offer vital guidance for formulating evidence-based interventions aimed at fostering resilience and adaptive behaviors in the face of diverse environmental challenges.

MECHANISMS OF EMOTIONAL CONDITIONING

Classical Conditioning - Fundamental Processes

1. Pioneers and Key Experiments:

Apart from Ivan Pavlov, the father of classical conditioning and previously discussed in this book, there were a few psychologists who also contributed to the development and refinement of this theory with their insights. One such figure is Robert Rescorla, whose pivotal research emphasized the significance of contingency and expectancy in associative learning. Through his investigations, Rescorla demonstrated that the predictability of an unconditioned stimulus following a conditioned stimulus profoundly influences the strength and persistence of conditioning. His work elucidated the nuanced nature of stimulus relationships, challenging prior assumptions about the deterministic nature of classical conditioning. By refocusing attention on the role of cognitive processes in conditioning, Rescorla's contributions broadened the theoretical framework of behavioral psychology and stimulated new directions in research and theory.

On the other hand, Mary Cover Jones also made noteworthy advancements by applying classical conditioning principles in therapeutic interventions, particularly in the treatment of phobias. Her compassionate and methodical work with Peter, a young boy with a severe rabbit phobia, showcased the effectiveness of systematic desensitization—a technique that gradually exposed individuals to feared stimuli while promoting relaxation. Jones's pioneering application of classical conditioning as a means of treating maladaptive emotional responses is emblematic of the profound impact of psychological research on practical domains.

2. Mechanisms of Stimulus Association:

The process of stimulus association underlies the formation of an emotional response to a previously neutral stimulus. This mechanism involves the pairing of an unconditioned stimulus (UCS), which naturally elicits a specific response, with a neutral stimulus (NS) that initially does not elicit the same response. Through repeated pairings, the NS becomes a conditioned stimulus (CS) capable of eliciting a similar response as the UCS. One of the key mechanisms underlying this association is the temporal contiguity between the presentation of the NS and the UCS. The closer the pairing in time, the stronger the association becomes. Additionally, the predictability of the NS preceding the UCS enhances the strength of the association. This predictive value allows for the anticipatory nature of the conditioned response.

Further, the concept of stimulus relevance is crucial in understanding the mechanisms of association. Not all stimuli are equally likely to become associated, and factors such as biological preparedness and attention play pivotal roles in determining which stimuli will form strong associations. Biologically prepared stimuli are those that are inherently more likely to be linked with certain responses due to evolutionary and survival significance. Moreover, attentional processes enhance the likelihood of forming an association by increasing the perceptual salience of the stimuli involved. Attention focuses cognitive resources on the relevant stimuli, allowing for more effective learning and association.

Understanding the neural mechanisms underlying stimulus association is another important aspect of this process. The brain regions involved in stimulus association, such as the amygdala and hippocampus, play vital roles in encoding the emotional significance of stimuli, consolidating the learned associations, and retrieving the conditioned responses when encountering the CS. Neurotransmitter systems, particularly those involving dopamine and serotonin, modulate the strength of the associations and the expression of conditioned responses.

Recent research has focused on the role of higher-order cognitive processes, such as expectancy and evaluative conditioning, in shaping the mechanisms of stimulus association. Expectancy refers to the anticipation of the UCS following the CS, and variations in expectancy can lead to different patterns of conditioning. Evaluative conditioning, on the other hand, involves the transfer of the emotional value of one stimulus to another through associative learning processes, leading to changes in the emotional significance of the CS. Understanding these higher-order processes provides a more comprehensive view of the complexity of stimulus association in classical conditioning.

3. Phases of Conditioning:

In classical conditioning, the process of learning occurs in distinct phases, each with its own significant implications for behavior. The initial phase, known as acquisition, involves the association between a neutral stimulus and an unconditioned stimulus. This phase is characterized by the gradual strengthening of the conditioned response as the neutral stimulus becomes a reliable predictor of the unconditioned stimulus. The phenomena of acquisition highlight the fundamental principle of contingency, where the occurrence of the unconditioned stimulus depends on the presence of the conditioned stimulus. Understanding the precise mechanisms underlying acquisition is crucial for comprehending how new emotional responses are formed and consolidated.

Extinction, the subsequent phase, entails the diminishing of the conditioned response when the conditioned stimulus is presented without the unconditioned stimulus. This process reflects the reduction in the predictive value of the conditioned stimulus, leading to the eventual suppression of the learned response. Exploring extinction illuminates the delicate balance between learned associations and the modification of behavior in ever-changing environments. Moreover, the study of extinction provides insights into the potential for inhibiting maladaptive emotional responses through targeted interventions and exposure therapies.

Following extinction, the phenomenon of recovery represents the resurgence of the conditioned response after a period of rest or following the reintroduction of the unconditioned stimulus. This resurgence raises intriguing questions about the persistence of conditioned associations and the factors contributing to their reemergence. Investigating recovery sheds light on the durability of conditioned emotional responses and the intricacies involved in their modulation over time.

By comprehensively examining the phases of conditioning – acquisition, extinction, and recovery – researchers and practitioners gain a nuanced understanding of the dynamic interplay between environmental cues and emotional reactions. Furthermore, this knowledge forms the basis for developing effective strategies to modify ingrained emotional responses and foster adaptive behavior in individuals across diverse contexts.

4. The Role of Timing and Frequency in Conditioning:

The precise temporal relationship between the conditioned stimulus (CS) and the unconditioned stimulus (US) is a critical determinant of conditioning efficacy. In the initial stages of acquisition, the contingency between the CS and the US establishes the temporal parameters within which learning occurs. Short-delay and trace conditioning, where the onset of the CS precedes or overlaps with the onset of the US, are often associated with robust conditioning effects due to the close temporal contiguity. These paradigms allow for optimal association between the two stimuli, facilitating the formation of a strong conditioned response.

Conversely, long-delay and backward conditioning - characterized by a considerable temporal gap and the presentation of the CS following the US, respectively - tend to yield weaker and less reliable conditioning outcomes. The elongated interval between the CS and the US diminishes the salience of their connection, impeding the establishment of a robust conditioned response. Understanding the temporal dynamics of conditioning is imperative in elucidating the underlying processes that govern associative learning, offering insights into how timing influences the encoding and retrieval of conditioned associations.

The frequency of pairing between the CS and the US profoundly influences the rate of acquisition and the persistence of conditioned responses. High-frequency pairings, wherein the CS consistently precedes the US, promote rapid learning and robust conditioning. The repeated exposure to the CS-US contingency strengthens the association between the stimuli, solidifying the conditioned response. Conversely, low-frequency pairings may result in slower acquisition and weaker conditioning, as the infrequent occurrence of the CS-US pairing impedes the consolidation of the learned association.

Variations in the inter-trial intervals between successive presentations of the CS and the US can modulate the efficacy of conditioning. Optimal inter-stimulus intervals, reflective of the temporal relationship between the CS and the US, are fundamental in shaping the temporal contingencies that underpin classical conditioning. These intervals not only influence the strength of the conditioned response but also impact the generalization and discrimination capabilities of the organism, thereby delineating the boundaries within which the conditioned response is elicited.

5. Generalization, Discrimination, and Compound Stimuli:

Generalization, discrimination, and compound stimuli delineate how organisms respond to similar stimuli, differentiate between stimuli, and process multiple stimuli in complex environments. Generalization refers to the tendency of a conditioned response to occur not only to the original conditioned stimulus but also to other stimuli that are similar to it. This phenomenon highlights the broadening of the response to encompass a range of stimuli with shared features, emphasizing the adaptive nature of conditioning. However, discrimination presents an equally intriguing aspect of response specificity, as it involves the capacity to differentiate between similar stimuli and produce the conditioned response only to the original stimulus while withholding it from others. The interplay between generalization and discrimination underscores the nature of stimulus processing and response modulation in conditioned behavior. Moreover, the introduction of compound stimuli further illustrates the multifaceted nature of stimulus integration in conditioning. When two or more stimuli are presented together to elicit a response, the resulting interaction can yield distinct behavioral outcomes that may differ from responses to individual stimuli. Understanding the mechanisms of compound stimuli is vital in elucidating the complexities of real-world situations where multiple cues co-occur and influence behavior. Through empirical studies and theoretical frameworks, researchers have delved into the nuances of generalization, discrimination, and compound stimuli to unravel the underlying cognitive processes and neural mechanisms governing these phenomena. Exploring practical applications, such as behavioral therapies and animal training, has underscored the significance of these concepts in shaping learning paradigms and influencing behavioral interventions. By comprehensively examining the interplay of these concepts, a deeper understanding of the breadth and depth of classical conditioning emerges, illuminating the ways in which organisms perceive, process, and respond to environmental cues.

6. Biological Predispositions in Classical Conditioning:

Classical conditioning has provided significant insights into the mechanisms underlying learned associations between stimuli. However, an intriguing aspect of classical conditioning lies in the varying degrees to which organisms exhibit predispositions to acquire certain conditioned responses. These biological predispositions play a crucial role in shaping the course of learning and are of particular interest in understanding emotional and psychological phenomena.

Central to the concept of biological predispositions in classical conditioning is the idea that not all stimuli are equally likely to become associated with specific responses. Evolutionary psychologists have proposed that the predisposition to form certain associations can be linked to the survival advantage conferred by rapid learning of potentially harmful or beneficial stimuli. For instance, research on fear conditioning in animals has shown that aversive conditioning to stimuli such as snakes or spiders occurs more readily than to neutral stimuli, suggesting an evolved predisposition to respond to threat-related cues.

Studies on taste aversion conditioning have revealed that organisms are more likely to develop an aversion to novel tastes rather than novel sights or sounds, highlighting the influence of evolutionary pressures on learning. This phenomenon aligns with the adaptive significance of quickly associating new tastes with potential toxicity, thereby increasing the likelihood of survival.

In addition to evolutionary considerations, researchers have delved into the neurobiological underpinnings of biological predispositions in classical conditioning. Findings from neuroimaging studies and experiments utilizing animal models have uncovered neural pathways and neurotransmitter systems that confer differential susceptibility to conditioned associations. For example, the amygdala, a key structure involved in emotional processing, has been implicated in the rapid acquisition of fear responses to evolutionarily relevant stimuli.

The interplay between genetic factors and environmental influences in shaping predispositions to classical conditioning has garnered attention. Twin studies and genetic knockout experiments have provided evidence for heritable components influencing the likelihood of forming specific conditioned responses, shedding light on the complex interplay between genetic predispositions and experiential factors in learning.

Understanding biological predispositions in classical conditioning holds implications for various domains, including clinical psychology, education, and behavioral interventions. By recognizing the inherent differences in individuals' propensity to acquire certain associations, personalized approaches to therapeutic interventions and educational strategies can be tailored to better accommodate diverse learning profiles. Moreover, insights into biological predispositions contribute to the broader understanding of how environmental and genetic factors interact in shaping behavioral and emotional responses, offering a nuanced perspective on the complexities of human and animal learning.

7. Emotional Responses Elicited through Conditioning:

Emotional responses elicited through conditioning represent a fascinating intersection of psychological and physiological processes. Classical conditioning, in particular, has provided significant insight into how individuals develop emotional reactions to specific stimuli based on their associative learning experiences. Central to the discussion is the concept of emotional salience, where certain stimuli acquire heightened emotional significance through repeated pairing with unconditioned stimuli. For instance, the classic case of Pavlov's dogs demonstrates how neutral stimuli, such as the sound of a bell, can become associated with the delivery of food, ultimately evoking a conditioned response of salivation in anticipation of the food. This process illuminates the manner in which emotional responses can be elicited through learned associations, paving the way for an enhanced comprehension of how individuals develop fears, phobias, and other emotional reactions within their environments.

The role of context in shaping emotional responses cannot be overlooked. The environmental cues accompanying conditioned stimuli contribute to the robustness and specificity of emotional conditioning, influencing when and how these responses are expressed. Understanding the contextual influences on emotional conditioning provides valuable insights into the adaptive nature of emotional responses and the potential avenues for targeted interventions in instances of maladaptive emotional reactions.

It is imperative to delve into the implications of emotional conditioning for emotional regulation and psychopathology. By elucidating the processes through which emotional responses are elicited and modulated through conditioning, researchers and practitioners gain actionable knowledge for therapeutic approaches aimed at mitigating the impact of aversive conditioning experiences. Additionally, this exploration opens up avenues for examining how emotional conditioning intersects with individual differences, developmental factors, and sociocultural contexts to shape the diversity of emotional responses observed across populations.

8. Challenges and Critiques:

When it comes to classical conditioning, one of the primary criticisms revolves around the oversimplification of complex emotional phenomena. Critics argue that the deterministic nature of classical conditioning fails to account for the intricacies of human emotions, which are often influenced by cognitive, social, and cultural factors. Additionally, the focus on observable stimuli and responses overlooks the subjective experiences and internal mental processes that shape emotional behavior. Another challenge pertains to the generalization of findings from controlled laboratory settings to real-world contexts. Critics assert that the artificiality of experimental conditions limits the applicability of classical conditioning principles to natural environments, where emotions are subject to multifaceted influences. Furthermore, ethical considerations arise concerning the use of aversive conditioning techniques, such as fear induction, and the potential psychological harm it may cause. Critics raise concerns about the implications of exploiting emotional vulnerability for experimental purposes, emphasizing the need for responsible and humane treatment of participants. Moreover, contemporary critiques point to the limitations of classical conditioning in accounting for individual differences in emotional reactivity and resilience. The one-size-fits-all approach of classical conditioning overlooks the diverse psychological makeup of individuals, leading to questions about the universality of conditioned emotional responses. Additionally, the temporal stability of conditioned emotional reactions has been questioned, with some researchers arguing that the durability of such responses may be less enduring than previously assumed. These critiques prompt a reevaluation of the scope and applicability of classical conditioning in understanding the complexities of emotional behavior. Addressing these challenges requires an integrative approach that considers the interplay of biological, psychological, and social factors in shaping emotional responses. It necessitates a shift towards interdisciplinary research that encompasses cognitive and affective processes, thereby enriching our understanding of the mechanisms underlying human emotions.

9. Implications for Understanding Emotional Behavior:

Classical conditioning holds significant implications for understanding emotional behavior and human psychology. One key implication pertains to the formation and modification of emotional responses. Through classical conditioning, individuals can develop conditioned emotional reactions to previously neutral stimuli, a process that underpins the acquisition of fears, phobias, and other emotional associations. Understanding these mechanisms is crucial in addressing maladaptive emotional behaviors and designing appropriate interventions to alleviate emotional distress.

Classical conditioning offers insights into the role of context and environmental cues in shaping emotional experiences. The study of contextual conditioning underscores the influential impact of situational factors on emotional reactivity and affective responses. This has profound implications for individuals dealing with anxiety, stress, or trauma, as it highlights the potential for environmental modifications to mitigate negative emotional triggers and promote emotional well-being.

An additional implication lies in the domain of therapeutic interventions and behavior modification. Drawing from classical conditioning principles, clinicians and psychologists can employ systematic desensitization, aversion therapy, and exposure-based treatments to address emotional disorders and maladaptive behaviors. By leveraging the processes of extinction and reconditioning, these interventions aim to alter emotional responses and facilitate adaptive coping strategies in individuals grappling with emotional challenges.

The examination of biological predispositions in classical conditioning sheds light on the interplay between genetic influences and emotional learning. Understanding how certain individuals may be more predisposed to develop specific conditioned responses provides valuable insight into the heterogeneity of emotional behaviors and informs personalized approaches to emotional regulation and treatment.

Operant Conditioning and Reinforcement Models

1. Historical Development of Reinforcement Models:

During the early to mid-20th century, the conceptualization of reinforcement underwent significant advancements, leading to the establishment of key theoretical frameworks that continue to shape contemporary behavioral science. Skinner's experiments with pigeons and rats demonstrated the powerful influence of reinforcement on shaping behavior, providing empirical evidence for the effectiveness of this approach. These seminal studies paved the way for the formalization and refinement of reinforcement models, marking a crucial turning point in the history of behavioral psychology. The emergence of reinforcement theory represented a departure from purely reflexive or respondent behaviors, highlighting the importance of environmental consequences in modulating voluntary actions. Researchers grappled with the complexities of reinforcement paradigms, delving into the nuances of positive and negative reinforcement, punishment, and schedules of reinforcement. This in-depth exploration led to the formulation of detailed taxonomies and classifications, illuminating the multifaceted nature of reinforcement processes. Over time, the field witnessed the integration of reinforcement concepts into diverse domains, including education, clinical psychology, and organizational behavior. The legacy of historical figures such as Skinner and the subsequent wave of behavioral scientists has left an indelible imprint on the evolution of reinforcement models. Their collective contributions have shaped the landscape of modern behavior analysis and continue to inspire innovative research in understanding and modifying human behavior.

2. Core Principles of Operant Conditioning:

The core principles of operant conditioning, first introduced by B.F. Skinner, revolve around the idea that behaviors are influenced by their consequences. In other words, individuals tend to repeat behaviors that are followed by favorable outcomes while avoiding those that lead to unfavorable consequences. This fundamental process shapes the learning and adaptation of individuals across various contexts.

At the heart of operant conditioning are the concepts of reinforcement and punishment. Reinforcement refers to the process of strengthening a particular behavior by providing a consequence that increases the likelihood of its recurrence. On the other hand, punishment involves applying a consequence that decreases the likelihood of a behavior being repeated. Both reinforcement and punishment play pivotal roles in shaping and modifying behaviors, forming the building blocks of operant conditioning.

Another critical element of operant conditioning is the distinction between positive and negative reinforcement/punishment. Positive reinforcement involves presenting a desirable stimulus following a behavior, thereby reinforcing it. Conversely, negative reinforcement entails the removal of an aversive stimulus, leading to an increase in the likelihood of the behavior being repeated. Similarly, positive punishment involves adding an undesirable consequence, while negative punishment entails removing a valued stimulus, both resulting in a decrease in the probability of the behavior occurring again.

Schedules of reinforcement contribute significantly to the effectiveness of operant conditioning. These schedules, including continuous reinforcement and intermittent reinforcement, impact the rate and persistence of learned behaviors. Understanding how different reinforcement schedules influence behavior is crucial in various real-world applications, from education and parenting to organizational management and clinical interventions.

Operant conditioning emphasizes the role of context and timing in shaping behavioral responses. The temporal relationship between behavior and its consequence, as well as the environmental setting in which learning takes place, greatly influences the effectiveness of operant conditioning techniques. Recognizing the contextual factors that impact behavior allows for more precise application of operant conditioning principles, maximizing their efficacy in behavioral modification efforts.

3. Types of Reinforcement:

Reinforcement can be broadly classified into two categories: positive reinforcement and negative reinforcement. Positive reinforcement involves the presentation of a desirable stimulus following a specific behavior, thereby increasing the likelihood of that behavior being repeated in the future. For instance, providing praise to a child for completing their homework can serve as a positive reinforcement, encouraging them to continue such diligent behavior. This form of reinforcement operates on the principle of reward, whereby the introduction of a favorable outcome strengthens the association between the behavior and its consequences.

Conversely, negative reinforcement entails the removal or avoidance of an aversive stimulus to strengthen the occurrence of a particular behavior. By escaping or avoiding an unpleasant situation or stimulus, individuals are more likely to engage in behaviors that lead to the elimination of such discomfort. An example of negative reinforcement is a student studying diligently in order to avoid the stress and anxiety associated with failing an exam. Both positive and negative reinforcement play pivotal roles in influencing behavioral patterns and learning processes among individuals across diverse contexts.

It is important to note that while positive reinforcement focuses on adding something desirable, negative reinforcement centers on removing something undesirable. These distinct forms of reinforcement demonstrate the dynamic nature of operant conditioning and underscore the nuanced ways in which behaviors are shaped and sustained through environmental contingencies. Understanding the differential impacts of positive and negative reinforcement is instrumental in designing effective behavioral interventions, educational strategies, and therapeutic approaches.

The comprehensive grasp of reinforcement theories enhances our insight into the complex mechanisms underlying human and animal behavior. By delving into the intricacies of reinforcement and its manifold applications, we gain valuable perspectives on motivational dynamics, self-regulation processes, and the cultivation of adaptive behaviors. Equipped with this knowledge, practitioners and researchers can devise tailored interventions that leverage the power of reinforcement to promote positive change and foster resilient behavioral patterns.

4. Schedules of Reinforcement and Their Effects:

Schedules of reinforcement shape the frequency and strength of learned behaviors. Psychologists have extensively studied these schedules to understand their effects on behavior and motivation. The two main categories of reinforcement schedules are continuous and intermittent. Continuous reinforcement involves rewarding a behavior every time it occurs, which can result in rapid learning but also rapid extinction when the reinforcement is removed. In contrast, intermittent reinforcement only rewards the behavior some of the time, leading to more persistent behavior even in the absence of reinforcement. Various types of intermittent schedules exist, including fixed ratio, variable ratio, fixed interval, and variable interval schedules. Each schedule has unique effects on behavior. Fixed ratio schedules reinforce behavior after a specific number of responses, often resulting in high rates of responding with brief pauses after reinforcement. Variable ratio schedules reinforce behavior after an unpredictable number of responses, leading to consistently high rates of responding as seen in gambling or sales environments. Fixed interval schedules reinforce the first response after a fixed time interval, resulting in a scalloped pattern of responding with increased rates closer to the reinforcement delivery time. Variable interval schedules reinforce the first response after varying time intervals, promoting consistent, steady rates of responding. Understanding these diverse reinforcement schedules is crucial for analyzing behavioral patterns in various contexts, from clinical interventions to organizational management. Furthermore, the effects of these schedules can provide insights into addictive behaviors, persistence in the face of adversity, and the development of maladaptive behaviors.

5. Punishment:

Punishment in the context of operant conditioning refers to the introduction of an aversive stimulus or the removal of a reinforcing stimulus in response to a behavior, with the intent of decreasing the likelihood of that behavior occurring again. One of the primary controversies surrounding punishment within the sphere of operant conditioning is the ethical considerations and potential detrimental effects it may have on an individual's psychological well-being. While the immediate suppression of targeted behaviors may be achieved through punishment, research has shown that it often fails as a long-term strategy for behavioral change. Additionally, the use of punishment raises poignant questions regarding human dignity and autonomy, provoking debates about the balance between behavioral control and individual agency.

The concept of punishment does not exist in isolation, and its effectiveness must be analyzed in comparison to reinforcement strategies. The application of punishment also extends beyond individual behavior to broader societal systems, such as the criminal justice system. This leads to complex discussions about the role of punishment in shaping societal norms, legal frameworks, and the implications for social justice. Delving into historical and contemporary perspectives, the controversies surrounding punitive measures are critically evaluated within the context of fostering positive behavioral change while considering the potential collateral consequences on diverse populations and communities.

6. Operant Conditioning in Emotional Contexts:

Emotional conditioning through operant processes occurs when an individual's behavior is shaped by its consequences in an emotionally charged environment. Reinforcement of certain emotional responses can lead to their amplification, while punishment may suppress or modify undesirable emotional behaviors. For instance, in a therapeutic setting, positive reinforcement can be used to bolster adaptive emotional responses, such as assertiveness or empathy, while negative punishment might be employed to discourage maladaptive emotional outbursts or aggression.

Operant conditioning in emotional contexts extends beyond individual experiences to social and cultural influences. The reinforcement of specific emotional displays within a social group or community can significantly impact an individual's emotional repertoire. Through operant conditioning, social norms and expectations regarding emotional expression are ingrained, shaping how individuals perceive and respond to their own and others' emotions within various social settings. This interplay between operant conditioning and emotional expression highlights the complex nature of emotional regulation and underscores the importance of considering social and cultural factors in understanding emotional behaviors.

The emotional impact of operant conditioning is evident in diverse domains, including education, workplace dynamics, and clinical interventions. In educational settings, teachers employ various reinforcement strategies to promote desirable emotional responses and engagement in learning activities. By utilizing positive reinforcement, educators can foster enthusiasm and perseverance, contributing to a conducive learning environment.

Conversely, punishment-based approaches may inadvertently create anxiety or aversion towards specific subjects or classroom interactions.

In work environments, operant conditioning principles influence employee motivation and emotional well-being. Through performance appraisals, incentive systems, and feedback mechanisms, organizations shape employees' emotional experiences and behaviors at work. Positive reinforcement for exemplary performance can enhance job satisfaction and commitment, whereas punitive measures may generate stress and disengagement, ultimately impacting the overall organizational climate.

Within clinical settings, operant conditioning techniques are utilized to address emotional disturbances and maladaptive behaviors. Behavior modification programs often incorporate reinforcement schedules to encourage desired emotional regulation and diminish dysfunctional expressions. By systematically reinforcing adaptive emotional responses and providing alternative coping mechanisms, clinicians endeavor to reshape emotional patterns and alleviate distress.

Overall, the multifaceted interplay between operant conditioning and emotional contexts underscores the pervasive influence of environmental contingencies on emotional experiences and behaviors. Understanding these dynamics is essential for leveraging operant conditioning principles to cultivate emotionally healthy and adaptive individuals within diverse societal and institutional frameworks.

7. Theoretical Debates and Criticisms:

Operant conditioning and reinforcement models have been the subject of extensive theoretical debates and criticisms within the field of psychology. One of the primary areas of contention revolves around the concept of punishment and its efficacy in modifying behavior. Critics argue that punishment, particularly in the form of aversive stimuli, may lead to negative emotional and psychological effects, undermining the overall well-being of the individual undergoing such interventions. Furthermore, the ethical implications of utilizing punishment in behavioral modification strategies have sparked intense discussions within both academic and clinical settings. Proponents of operant conditioning, on the other hand, assert that carefully administered punishment can be effective in curbing undesirable behaviors, especially when paired with positive reinforcement for desirable alternatives.

Another significant theoretical debate pertains to the relative importance of positive and negative reinforcement in shaping behavior. While traditional views emphasize the role of positive reinforcement in increasing the likelihood of desired behaviors, some contemporary theorists argue that the avoidance of aversive stimuli (negative reinforcement) plays an equally crucial role in behavioral acquisition. This ongoing discourse reflects the dynamic nature of theoretical frameworks in operant conditioning and reinforces the need for continued empirical research to elucidate the nuanced mechanisms underlying reinforcement processes.

In addition to internal theoretical debates, criticisms of operant conditioning also extend to its application in real-world settings. Detractors raise concerns about the potential oversimplification of human behavior within the context of reinforcement models, positing that the interplay of cognitive, emotional, and social factors may not be adequately captured by these behaviorist paradigms alone. Furthermore, the limitations of generalizing findings from controlled laboratory experiments to complex, naturalistic environments have prompted calls for a more comprehensive understanding of the contextual factors influencing operant behaviors.

The societal implications of employing operant conditioning techniques in various domains, including education, parenting, and organizational management, have drawn attention to the broader ethical and cultural considerations associated with behavior modification. The divergent perspectives on the ethical use of reinforcement strategies underscore the imperative of incorporating multifaceted ethical analyses into the implementation of operant conditioning interventions.

8. Implications for Future Research and Practice:

As we explore the implications for future research and practice in the sphere of operant conditioning and reinforcement models, it becomes evident that there are several promising avenues for further exploration and application. One key area for future research lies in the continued examination of individual differences in responsiveness to reinforcement and punishment paradigms. Understanding the factors that influence variation in behavioral responses can shed light on the development of personalized interventions that are tailored to individuals' specific needs.

The integration of technology into behavioral research and practice presents a rich field for exploration. Innovations in data collection, analysis, and intervention delivery offer unprecedented opportunities to refine our understanding of operant conditioning processes and to develop more effective, efficient, and accessible interventions. For instance, the use of advanced data analytics and machine learning algorithms can provide valuable insights into complex behavioral patterns and facilitate the identification of optimal reinforcement strategies.

Addressing the practical implications, the future of operant conditioning research holds the potential to significantly impact diverse domains, such as education, healthcare, and organizational management. By leveraging the insights gained from ongoing research, educators can design instructional programs that maximize positive reinforcement and minimize punitive measures, thereby enhancing learning outcomes and fostering a positive classroom environment. In healthcare settings, the application of operant conditioning principles can inform the development of behavior modification strategies to support patients in adhering to treatment regimens and adopting healthier lifestyle behaviors.

Within the sphere of organizational management, the nuanced understanding of reinforcement models can guide leaders in shaping environments that motivate employees, cultivate desirable work habits, and foster a culture of continuous improvement. Moreover, the integration of ethical considerations and the proactive mitigation of unintended consequences remain crucial focal points for ensuring that future applications of operant conditioning adhere to the highest standards of professional conduct and social responsibility.

Observational Learning and Emotional Imprinting

1. Introduction to Observational Learning:

Observational learning, a key concept in the field of behavioral psychology, delves into the processes through which individuals acquire new behaviors by observing and imitating others. This form of learning is deeply intertwined with social cognition and holds substantial relevance in understanding the development and transmission of emotional responses. At its core, observational learning emphasizes the power of modeling and imitation as fundamental mechanisms for adopting new behaviors within a social context. While traditional forms of learning center around direct experiences and explicit instruction, observational learning expands our understanding of how individuals can learn indirectly through the observation of others. Through this process, individuals are not merely passive recipients of information, but active processors and interpreters of observed behaviors. The theoretical foundations of observational learning draw insights from cognitive, social, and developmental psychology, integrating perspectives to elucidate the intricacies of how individuals learn from their social environment. From early foundational studies by psychologists like Albert Bandura to contemporary research exploring the neural underpinnings of social learning, the exploration of observational learning has offered profound insights into the dynamics of human behavior. Moreover, observational learning provides a crucial framework for comprehending the transmission of emotional responses within social groups, shedding light on how individuals develop and internalize emotional patterns from their interactions with others. As such, gaining a comprehensive understanding of observational learning is paramount in unraveling the complexities of emotional imprinting and the acquisition of affective behaviors.

2. Theoretical Foundations of Emotional Imprinting:

Emotional imprinting is a critical concept that elucidates the process through which individuals form lasting emotional associations, often in early life, based on the cues and behaviors exhibited by significant others in their environment. This mechanism, initially proposed by Konrad Lorenz in the sphere of ethology, has garnered substantial attention across various disciplines for its implications in understanding emotional development and social behavior. At its core, emotional imprinting revolves around the idea that young organisms are particularly susceptible to learning and internalizing emotional responses from caregivers or conspecifics. This phenomenon is believed to have profound and enduring impacts on an individual's emotional repertoire and bonding patterns throughout their lifespan. The theoretical framework of emotional imprinting integrates principles from psychology, ethology, and neuroscience to offer a comprehensive understanding of how emotional experiences shape an individual's cognitive and affective processes. As such, it encompasses elements of socioemotional development, attachment theories, and the neural substrates involved in emotional memory and processing. Furthermore, this conceptual model underscores the interplay between genetic predispositions and environmental influences in shaping emotional reactivity and adaptive behavioral strategies. Notably, researchers have investigated the role of epigenetic mechanisms in modulating the expression of emotional imprints, thereby shedding light on the interplay between nature and nurture in emotional development. Moreover, theoretical perspectives on emotional imprinting extend beyond the scope of individual psychology to encompass broader societal implications, particularly in the context of cultural transmission and intergenerational continuity of emotional norms and behaviors.

3. Pioneers and Key Experiments:

The exploration of observational learning owes much to the contributions of several eminent pioneers in the field of psychology. Albert Bandura, the father of social learning theory (later known as social cognitive theory), was instrumental in elucidating the principles of observational learning through his groundbreaking experiments. Bandura's seminal work, particularly his notable Bobo doll experiment conducted in 1961, revealed the significant impact of observational learning on emotional responses and behavior. The innovative design of this experiment involved exposing children to aggressive behavior modeled by an adult towards a Bobo doll. Bandura demonstrated that children who observed the aggressive actions were more likely to replicate similar behaviors when given the opportunity. This pivotal research shed light on the profound influence of observational learning in shaping emotional responses and imprinting behavioral patterns. Another influential figure in the study of observational learning is Julian Rotter, whose pioneering investigations delved into the mechanisms of social learning and the role of reinforcement in observational processes. Through meticulously designed experiments, Rotter elucidated how individuals acquire emotional reactions and adaptive behaviors by observing the consequences experienced by others. His seminal contributions have profoundly influenced our understanding of how observational learning contributes to emotional development and adaptive functioning. Furthermore, the work of Neal Miller and John Dollard has been instrumental in delineating the processes underlying observational learning and emotional imprinting. Their comprehensive studies emphasized the interplay between external cues, cognitive processes, and emotional responses in observational contexts, laying a robust theoretical foundation for subsequent research in this domain. Additionally, the groundbreaking experiments conducted by Mary Cover Jones, often regarded as the 'mother of behavior therapy,' significantly advanced our comprehension of observational learning and emotional conditioning. Her empirical investigations on the treatment of phobias in children paved the way for the application of observational learning principles in therapeutic interventions, showcasing the transformative potential of such approaches across diverse settings.

4. Mechanisms Underlying Imitation and Modeling:

Imitation and modeling are fundamental processes in observational learning, playing a crucial role in the acquisition and transmission of emotional responses and complex behaviors. The mechanisms underlying imitation and modeling involve intricate cognitive and neurobiological processes that facilitate social learning and adaptation. At a cognitive level, individuals engage in attentional processes to observe and encode the behavior of role models, which is crucial for successful imitation. This selective attention allows individuals to focus on relevant cues and actions, enhancing the likelihood of accurate reproduction of observed behaviors. Moreover, working memory and symbolic representation enable the retention of modeled behaviors, laying the foundation for their eventual reproduction. The encoding and storage of observed actions allow individuals to retrieve and reproduce them when appropriate, thereby consolidating the learned responses. In addition to cognitive processes, neurobiological mechanisms underpinning imitation and modeling include mirror neurons and neural resonance systems. Mirror neurons, primarily found in the premotor cortex and parietal cortex, activate both when an individual performs a specific action and when they observe another individual engaging in the same action. This mirroring phenomenon provides a neurological basis for understanding others' actions and intentions, facilitating the imitation of observed behaviors. Furthermore, neural resonance enables individuals to empathize with others' emotional states and internalize observed affective responses, contributing to emotional imprinting and social learning. The interconnectedness of cognitive and neurobiological processes underscores the complexity and adaptability of imitation and modeling in observational learning. Understanding these mechanisms is critical for comprehending how individuals acquire and replicate emotional responses and behaviors through observational learning, with implications for various domains including psychology, education, and clinical practice.

5. The Impact of Social Context on Learning Processes:

Human beings are inherently social creatures, and much of our behavioral repertoire is acquired through interactions within our social environment. When examining the impact of social context on learning, it becomes evident that individuals often look to others as a source of information and guidance, especially in ambiguous or uncertain situations. This phenomenon, known as social learning, encompasses a wide array of behaviors, including imitation, modeling, and vicarious reinforcement.

Social context influences learning processes through various mechanisms. One such mechanism is the concept of social facilitation, where the presence of others can enhance an individual's performance on simple or well-rehearsed tasks. Conversely, social inhibition may occur in more complex or novel tasks when individuals are being observed or evaluated by others, leading to a decline in performance. These dynamics illustrate the interplay between social influences and learning outcomes.

The role of interpersonal relationships and group dynamics cannot be overstated in understanding the impact of social context on learning. Within social groups, individuals are exposed to diverse perspectives, attitudes, and behavioral patterns, creating opportunities for observational learning and the acquisition of emotional responses. The dynamics of social conformity, obedience, and peer influence further underscore the profound influence of social context on emotional imprinting and behavioral conditioning.

Cultural norms and societal values also exert a significant impact on the learning process. The transmission of cultural practices and traditions occurs largely through observational learning within the social context. As individuals observe and assimilate the behaviors and emotional expressions of others within their cultural milieu, they internalize prevalent norms and values, thereby shaping their emotional responses and behavioral tendencies.

6. Emotional Development Through Mimicry:

Emotional development through mimicry is a process by which individuals learn to express and regulate their emotions based on the observed behaviors of others. This phenomenon plays a crucial role in shaping social and emotional competencies from early childhood through adulthood. As humans, we are innately predisposed to imitate the actions and emotional expressions of those around us, especially during our formative years. Infants and young children, in particular, engage in facial mimicry, where they mirror the emotional expressions of their caregivers as a means of social bonding and acquiring emotional understanding. This process not only facilitates emotional attunement but also lays the groundwork for developing empathy and interpersonal skills. Moreover, by observing how others cope with and display various emotions, individuals acquire a repertoire of emotional responses that are integrated into their own behavioral and communicative patterns. Emotional mimicry extends beyond facial expressions to encompass body language, vocal intonations, and even contagion of emotional states. Adolescents and adults continue to refine their emotional mimicry abilities, adapting their behaviors based on social cues and contextual demands. Through ongoing exposure to diverse emotional displays within different social contexts, individuals continually expand their emotional lexicon and refine their emotional regulation strategies. It is important to note that emotional mimicry can have both adaptive and maladaptive implications. Positive emotional mimicry contributes to building rapport, fostering trust, and promoting prosocial behaviors, while inappropriate or excessive mimicry may lead to emotional exhaustion, lack of authenticity, and potential emotional over-involvement. Understanding the dynamics of emotional mimicry is essential in various fields, including psychology, education, counseling, and interpersonal communication. By recognizing the interplay between observation, imitation, and emotional contagion, professionals can leverage these processes to facilitate emotional learning, promote positive behavior change, and enhance relational dynamics. The study of emotional development through mimicry underscores the significance of social learning in the cultivation of emotional intelligence and highlights the interconnectedness of individual and collective emotional experiences.

7. Challenges and Limitations in Observational Methods:

Despite their significance, it is imperative to acknowledge the inherent challenges and limitations associated with observational methods. One of the primary challenges in observational research is the issue of observer bias. Human observers may unintentionally inject their subjective interpretations into the data collection process, leading to potential distortions in the findings. Additionally, the presence of the observer can influence the behavior of the observed individuals, thereby compromising the naturalistic aspect of the study. This phenomenon, known as the Hawthorne effect, poses a significant challenge to the validity of observational data. Another critical limitation pertains to the ethical considerations surrounding privacy and consent. The use of video surveillance or naturalistic observation in public spaces raises concerns about invading individuals' privacy and autonomy. Researchers must address these ethical dilemmas meticulously to ensure that their studies uphold the principles of respect and beneficence. Furthermore, the generalizability of findings obtained from observational studies can be contentious. Cultural, social, and environmental factors greatly influence human behavior, and observations confined to specific contexts may not be universally applicable. This limitation accentuates the necessity of conducting comparative studies across diverse cultural contexts to discern the nuances of human behavior. Additionally, the lack of control over extraneous variables in naturalistic settings presents a noteworthy challenge. Unlike experimental settings, observational studies do not afford researchers the ability to manipulate and control all variables, thus posing difficulties in establishing causal relationships. Moreover, the reliance on qualitative data in observational research can introduce subjectivity and interpretation biases, necessitating rigorous methodological approaches to enhance the reliability and validity of the findings. In addressing these challenges, researchers must implement meticulous training for observers, employ rigorous coding and analysis techniques, and embrace interdisciplinary collaborations to enrich the interpretive frameworks. Despite these challenges and limitations, observational methods remain indispensable in unraveling the complexities of human behavior, emphasizing the need for continual refinement and innovation in their application.

8. Comparative Studies Across Cultural Contexts:

Culture plays a significant role in shaping the ways individuals perceive, express, and regulate their emotions. Comparative studies across various cultural contexts offer valuable insights into the diversity of emotional experiences and the influence of social norms, values, and practices on emotional development. By examining how different cultures interpret and respond to emotional stimuli, researchers can gain a deeper understanding of the universality versus cultural specificity of emotional processes.

One key focus of comparative studies is to explore the impact of cultural factors on emotional expression and recognition. For instance, some cultures may prioritize collective harmony and interdependence, leading to distinct patterns of emotional display and interpretation compared to cultures that emphasize individual autonomy. These cross-cultural variations can shed light on the fundamental mechanisms underlying emotional communication and provide a nuanced perspective on the sociocultural influences on emotional behaviors.

Additionally, comparative research delves into the role of cultural norms in shaping emotional regulation strategies. It investigates how cultural beliefs and practices influence the acceptance or suppression of specific emotions, as well as the effectiveness of various emotion regulation techniques within different cultural frameworks. Understanding these dynamics is crucial for developing culturally sensitive interventions and promoting emotional well-being across diverse populations.

Comparative studies often examine the manifestation of emotional disorders and psychopathology across cultures. By analyzing the prevalence, symptomatology, and explanatory models of mental health issues in various cultural contexts, researchers can identify the impact of cultural factors on the experience and expression of psychological distress. This knowledge informs the development of culturally relevant diagnostic criteria, therapeutic approaches, and support systems that align with the unique needs of different cultural groups.

Comparative studies allow for the exploration of cultural influences on emotional socialization and developmental trajectories. This includes investigating how children acquire emotional knowledge and regulation skills within their cultural milieu, as well as the transmission of cultural norms regarding emotional behavior through familial, educational, and societal channels. Recognizing the cultural embeddedness of emotional learning is essential for promoting emotionally intelligent and culturally competent practices in educational and clinical settings.

9. Implications for Therapeutic and Educational Settings:

The implications of observational learning and emotional imprinting for therapeutic and educational settings are far-reaching. Utilizing the principles of observational learning, therapists and educators can design interventions that leverage the power of modeling and imitation to facilitate positive behavioral change and emotional regulation in individuals. In therapeutic environments, the incorporation of observational learning techniques can enhance the effectiveness of cognitive-behavioral therapies, social skills training, and interventions aimed at addressing anxiety, phobias, and trauma-related disorders.

By strategically employing observational learning strategies, therapists can help individuals learn adaptive coping mechanisms by observing and imitating healthier behaviors demonstrated by others. This method can be particularly impactful for populations such as children, adolescents, and individuals with developmental or social communication challenges. Additionally, the integration of observational learning principles in therapeutic settings holds promise for promoting empathy, emotional understanding, and prosocial behaviors among clients.

Within educational settings, educators can use the insights from observational learning to optimize the learning environment. By creating opportunities for students to observe and model positive behaviors, teachers can foster a culture of mutual support, emotional resilience, and inclusive peer interactions. Through collaborative activities, role-playing exercises, and peer mentoring programs, students can develop essential socioemotional skills while internalizing constructive ways of managing their emotions and behaviors.

By acknowledging the influence of cultural contexts on observational learning and emotional imprinting, practitioners in both therapeutic and educational domains can tailor interventions to respect and integrate diverse cultural practices and norms, thus enhancing their relevance and effectiveness across different communities. It is important for professionals working in these settings to remain attuned to cultural nuances and adapt their approaches accordingly to ensure that interventions are holistic, culturally sensitive, and empowering.

Overall, the integration of observational learning and emotional imprinting in therapeutic and educational settings underscores the potential for promoting psychological well-being, fostering resilience, and nurturing emotionally intelligent individuals who can thrive in various social and academic contexts.

Neurobiological Underpinnings of Emotional Responses

1. Introduction to the Neurobiology of Emotions:

The exploration of neurobiology and emotions represents a fundamental cornerstone in understanding the mechanisms that underlie human behavior. In recent years, there has been a growing realization that emotions are not merely abstract concepts but are deeply rooted in the physiological and neurobiological processes of the human brain. Integrating the disciplines of neuroscience and emotional studies provides a comprehensive framework for unraveling the complex interplay between neural structures, biochemical pathways, and emotional responses.

At the core of this integrative approach lies the network of neural pathways responsible for emotion processing. Understanding the organization and connectivity of these pathways is instrumental in comprehending how emotional experiences are encoded, interpreted, and manifested within the human psyche.

The investigation into the neurobiology of emotions offers invaluable insights into the evolutionary roots of emotional experiences. By examining the phylogenetic conservation of neural substrates across species, we gain a deeper appreciation for the adaptive significance of emotions and their pervasive role in shaping survival behaviors. This cross-species perspective enables a broader comprehension of the universality and diversity of emotional expressions, transcending human-centric narratives to encompass a more holistic view of emotional phenomena.

Delving into the neurobiological basis of emotions allows for an examination of the impact of developmental processes on the formation of emotional circuits. The dynamic interplay between genetic predispositions and environmental influences shapes the structural and functional aspects of neural architecture, thereby sculpting an individual's emotional landscape. Unraveling the interweaving of nature and nurture in the context of emotional neurobiology opens avenues for understanding the vulnerabilities, resilience, and plasticity of emotional responses across the lifespan.

2. Neural Pathways Involved in Emotion Processing:

Emotions are complex, multifaceted phenomena that are intertwined with the functioning of the human brain. Understanding the neural pathways involved in emotion processing is crucial for unraveling the mysteries behind our emotional experiences. These pathways constitute a sophisticated network of interconnected structures and circuits that work in harmony to regulate and modulate our emotional responses. At the core of this system lies the limbic system, often referred to as the 'emotional brain'. The limbic system, comprising structures such as the amygdala, hippocampus, and hypothalamus, plays a pivotal role in processing and regulating emotions. It serves as a hub for integrating and interpreting sensory information, memories, and internal states to generate appropriate emotional responses. Additionally, the amygdala, known for its involvement in fear and threat processing, exerts profound influence on emotional reactivity and arousal. Beyond the limbic system, the prefrontal cortex and various cortical regions exert top-down regulatory control over emotional processes. The prefrontal cortex, particularly the ventromedial prefrontal cortex, is implicated in evaluating emotional stimuli and modulating emotional reactivity through cognitive appraisal. Furthermore, the interaction between subcortical and cortical structures within the amygdala-prefrontal circuitry governs the regulation of emotional responses and plays a critical role in emotional learning and memory. Additionally, the thalamus, acting as a relay station for sensory information, channels inputs to the amygdala and higher cortical areas, contributing to the rapid evaluation and processing of emotionally salient stimuli. These neural pathways are not isolated entities, but rather intertwined components of a dynamic system that orchestrate the perception, interpretation, and expression of emotions. A deeper comprehension of these pathways holds immense potential for elucidating the underlying mechanisms of emotional disorders and developing targeted interventions to alleviate emotional dysregulation. Moreover, advancements in neuroimaging techniques continue to unveil the complexities of these neural pathways, shedding light on the interplay between brain regions during emotional processing. As research in this field progresses, the web of neural pathways involved in emotion processing becomes increasingly decipherable, bringing us closer to unraveling the enigmatic nature of human emotions.

3. The Role of Neurotransmitters in Emotional Regulation:

Neurotransmitters, the chemical messengers of the nervous system, facilitate communication between neurons, shaping our perceptions, moods, and behaviors. Serotonin, a well-known neurotransmitter, is implicated in mood regulation, sleep, and appetite. Imbalances in serotonin levels have been linked to various emotional disorders, including depression and anxiety. Similarly, dopamine, another prominent neurotransmitter, influences our motivation, reward processing, and emotional arousal. Dysregulation of dopamine activity has been associated with conditions such as addiction and schizophrenia. Additionally, norepinephrine, which modulates attention, alertness, and stress responses, contributes to the regulation of emotional states. The interplay between these and other neurotransmitters highlights their significance in emotional processes. Understanding their function provides valuable insights into emotional dysregulation and the development of targeted interventions. Moreover, advances in neuropharmacology have led to the discovery of medications that modulate neurotransmitter activity, offering promising treatment options for individuals with emotional disorders. Furthermore, research exploring the interaction between neurotransmitters and cognitive-emotional functions sheds light on the underlying mechanisms of emotional regulation. This knowledge has far-reaching implications for clinical practice, informing the design of tailored therapeutic approaches and enhancing our comprehension of emotional well-being.

4. Impact of the Limbic System on Emotional Responses:

Comprising interconnected regions such as the amygdala, hippocampus, thalamus, and hypothalamus, the limbic system, a complex network of structures within the brain, orchestrates the processing and regulation of emotions. The amygdala, in particular, is recognized for its involvement in evaluating the emotional significance of stimuli and initiating appropriate behavioral and physiological responses. Its connections with sensory pathways allow for rapid detection and processing of potential threats or rewards, triggering fear or pleasure responses.

The hippocampus, integral to memory formation and retrieval, interacts closely with the amygdala in encoding emotional experiences and contextual details. This cross-talk influences the way in which past events and associated emotions are remembered and can impact future emotional reactions. Alongside the amygdala and hippocampus, the thalamus serves as a relay station for sensory information, channeling inputs to various cortical and subcortical regions for further processing and integration, thus influencing emotional perception and expression.

Additionally, the hypothalamus, a key regulator of autonomic and endocrine functions, modulates emotional responses through its influence on physiological processes such as heart rate, blood pressure, and hormone secretion. The interplay between the limbic system and these physiological mechanisms underscores the profound impact of emotional experiences on bodily states, reinforcing the bidirectional relationship between emotion and physical well-being.

The limbic system interfaces with higher cognitive processes mediated by the prefrontal cortex, allowing for the modulation and regulation of emotional reactivity and expression. This interaction enables individuals to engage in deliberative decision-making and adaptive responses, exerting control over impulsive or instinctual reactions. Dysfunction within this network can lead to difficulties in emotional regulation, contributing to mood disorders, anxiety, and impaired social functioning.

Understanding the workings of the limbic system sheds light on the neurobiological basis of emotional responses, highlighting the integrative nature of cognition, affect, and behavior. Moreover, insights into the impact of the limbic system provide valuable implications for therapeutic interventions targeting emotional dysregulation and psychopathology, offering hope for individuals grappling with the complexities of their emotional experiences.

5. Interactions Between Prefrontal Cortex and Emotional Control:

The prefrontal cortex, a region of the brain located at the front of the frontal lobe, plays a crucial role in regulating emotional responses and decision-making processes. Its intricate interactions with the limbic system, particularly the amygdala, form the neurobiological basis for emotional control and modulation. Through a complex network of connections, the prefrontal cortex modulates and regulates emotional responses, thereby influencing cognitive functions and behavior.

Studies have shown that the prefrontal cortex exerts inhibitory control over the amygdala, which is involved in processing emotions such as fear and aggression. This top-down regulation allows the prefrontal cortex to modulate the intensity of emotional responses and facilitate rational decision-making. Dysfunction or underdevelopment of the prefrontal cortex may lead to impairments in emotional regulation, resulting in difficulties in managing stress, impulse control, and social interactions.

The prefrontal cortex is involved in the appraisal and interpretation of emotional stimuli. It integrates sensory information with previous experiences and societal norms to evaluate the salience and significance of emotional cues. This process influences emotional perception and the generation of appropriate responses in various social contexts. Additionally, the prefrontal cortex contributes to the regulation of affective states, such as empathy, compassion, and emotional empathy, by integrating emotional and cognitive processes.

The prefrontal cortex is instrumental in exerting executive control over emotional impulses and adaptive decision-making. It facilitates the regulation of emotional responses through cognitive reappraisal, behavioral inhibition, and goal-directed behaviors. This ability to modulate emotions is essential for adaptive functioning in dynamic environments and interpersonal relationships.

Recent advances in neuroimaging techniques have provided valuable insights into the specific regions within the prefrontal cortex that are implicated in emotional control. The dorsolateral prefrontal cortex, ventromedial prefrontal cortex, and anterior cingulate cortex are among the key areas associated with emotion regulation and decision-making processes. These findings contribute to a better understanding of the neurobiological mechanisms underlying emotional control, paving the way for potential interventions targeting emotional dysregulation and related psychiatric disorders.

6. Genetic Predispositions and Their Influence on Emotional Responses:

Emotional responses are not solely the products of environmental influences; rather, they are shaped by a complex interplay of genetic and environmental factors. Genetic studies have identified certain gene variants that are associated with heightened emotional sensitivity or resilience. For instance, variations in genes responsible for neurotransmitter regulation, such as serotonin and dopamine, have been linked to differences in emotional processing and mood regulation. Additionally, the interaction between specific gene polymorphisms and early life experiences has been shown to significantly influence an individual's vulnerability to stress and propensity for emotional disorders.

Epigenetic mechanisms, which involve modifications to gene expression without altering the underlying DNA sequence, play a crucial role in mediating the impact of environmental stressors on emotional reactivity. Through epigenetic processes, environmental exposures can induce long-lasting changes in gene activity, contributing to the development of distinct emotional profiles among individuals.

Understanding the genetic underpinnings of emotional responses has far-reaching implications for personalized interventions and therapeutic approaches. By elucidating the genetic factors contributing to emotional vulnerabilities, clinicians can tailor treatment strategies to address the unique biological makeup of each individual. Moreover, insights gained from genetic research can inform the development of targeted pharmacological interventions that account for individual variations in drug response and efficacy.

However, it is essential to recognize that genetic influences do not operate in isolation and must be considered within the broader context of an individual's environmental experiences. The dynamic interplay between genetic predispositions and environmental influences underscores the need for a comprehensive, multidimensional approach to understanding and addressing emotional responses.

7. The Effects of Hormonal Changes on Emotions:

The endocrine system, comprising various glands that secrete hormones, interacts
with the brain to regulate emotions and behavior. Hormonal fluctuations, particularly those associated with stress and reproductive cycles, exert profound effects on emotional states. The hypothalamus, pituitary gland, and adrenal glands form a complex network known as the HPA axis, which is deeply involved in the body's response to stress and emotional arousal. When faced with stressors, the hypothalamus signals the pituitary gland to release adrenocorticotropic hormone (ACTH), which then stimulates the adrenal glands to produce cortisol, the primary stress hormone. Elevated levels of cortisol can influence mood,

motivation, and emotional reactivity. Furthermore, sex hormones such as estrogen and testosterone have been linked to emotional regulation. For instance, fluctuations in estrogen levels across the menstrual cycle have been associated with changes in mood and emotional sensitivity in women. Similarly, research suggests that testosterone influences aggression, dominance, and reward-related behaviors, all of which are intertwined with emotional experiences. Additionally, oxytocin and vasopressin, often referred to as the 'bonding hormones,' have been linked to social bonding, trust, empathy, and emotional empathy. These hormones facilitate social interactions and emotional expressions within interpersonal relationships. Moreover, the thyroid hormones, including thyroxine and triiodothyronine, govern metabolism and energy regulation, impacting emotional stability and cognitive functioning. Beyond their individual effects, these hormonal systems interact dynamically, influencing one another to orchestrate comprehensive emotional responses. Advances in neuroendocrinology have revealed the interplay between hormones and neurotransmitters, shedding light on how hormonal changes can shape emotional experiences at a neural level. Understanding the effects of hormonal changes on emotions is crucial in elucidating the multifaceted nature of human emotional responses and may have implications for developing targeted interventions to modulate emotional states in clinical settings.

8. Neuroplasticity and Adaptation in Emotional Conditioning:

Neuroplasticity refers to the brain's remarkable ability to reorganize itself by forming new neural connections throughout life. In the context of emotional conditioning, neuroplasticity enables individuals to adapt and learn from experiences, ultimately influencing their emotional reactions. Research has shown that emotional experiences can lead to structural changes in the brain, particularly in areas associated with emotion regulation such as the amygdala and prefrontal cortex. These changes may enhance or diminish the strength of emotional responses, depending on the nature of the conditioning. Understanding the mechanisms of neuroplasticity in emotional conditioning is essential for unraveling the complexities of human behavior and developing targeted interventions for emotional disorders. When individuals encounter emotionally challenging situations, their brains undergo synaptic plasticity, which involves the strengthening or weakening of neural connections. This process contributes to the formation of associative memories that shape future emotional responses. Furthermore, studies have demonstrated that prolonged exposure to certain emotions can lead to long-term alterations in neural circuitry, affecting an individual's overall emotional reactivity. The concept of neuroplasticity also underscores the potential for therapeutic interventions to modify maladaptive emotional responses. Interventions such as cognitive-behavioral therapy (CBT) capitalize on the brain's malleability to restructure maladaptive emotional patterns. By engaging in targeted exercises and behavioral modifications, individuals can effectively rewire their emotional pathways. It is evident that the dynamic nature of neuroplasticity in emotional conditioning holds significant implications for both clinical practice and everyday life. Moreover, emerging research in the field of neuroplasticity and emotional adaptation emphasizes the need for interdisciplinary approaches that integrate neurobiology, psychology, and clinical neuroscience. Collaborative efforts across these domains can lead to breakthroughs in understanding how the brain adapts to emotional stimuli and pave the way for personalized treatments tailored to individual neurobiological profiles.

9. Technological Advances in Neuroimaging and Emotional Studies:

Recent decades have witnessed remarkable strides in the field of neuroscience, particularly in the development of cutting-edge neuroimaging technologies that offer unprecedented insights into the workings of the human brain. These innovations have revolutionized the study of emotional responses by enabling researchers to explore the neural correlates of emotions with remarkable precision and detail. Among the most prominent neuroimaging techniques utilized in emotional studies are functional magnetic resonance imaging (fMRI), positron emission tomography (PET), magnetoencephalography (MEG), and near-infrared spectroscopy (NIRS), each offering unique advantages in capturing different aspects of emotional processing. fMRI, for instance, allows researchers to visualize changes in blood flow and oxygenation levels within the brain, providing valuable information on brain regions involved in emotional regulation and reactivity. PET, on the other hand, offers insights into neurotransmitter activity and receptor binding, shedding light on the neurochemical underpinnings of emotional responses. Furthermore, MEG enables the measurement of neuronal electrical activity with millisecond-level temporal resolution, while NIRS provides a non-invasive method for monitoring hemodynamic changes associated with emotional stimuli. The integration of these diverse neuroimaging modalities has led to a more comprehensive understanding of the neural circuits and mechanisms underlying emotional processes. Additionally, advancements in computational modeling and data analysis techniques have enhanced the interpretability of neuroimaging findings, allowing for sophisticated analyses of large-scale brain networks and dynamic interactions during emotional experiences. Furthermore, interdisciplinary collaborations between neuroscientists, psychologists, and computer scientists have fostered the development of innovative tools and methodologies for integrating neuroimaging data with behavioral and psychophysiological measures, enriching the scope and depth of emotional studies. As neuroimaging technologies continue to evolve, future prospects in emotional research hold immense promise, with emerging techniques such as functional connectivity MRI, diffusion tensor imaging, and real-time neurofeedback opening up new avenues for investigating the dynamic interplay between brain function and emotional states. Leveraging these advancements, researchers are poised to unravel the complexities of emotional regulation, vulnerability to psychological disorders, and individual differences in emotional processing, ultimately paving the way for targeted interventions and personalized therapeutic strategies in mental health care.

10. Integrative Perspectives on Neurobiological Mechanisms:

The intersection of neuroscience, psychology, and biology has shed light on the mechanisms governing how the brain processes and regulates emotions. This integration has not only deepened our comprehension of emotional experiences but also opened doors to potential interventions and treatments for emotional dysregulation and disorders.

One of the key takeaways from our discussion is the significance of technological advancements in neuroimaging and emotional studies. The ability to visualize and map brain activity associated with different emotional states has revolutionized our approach to studying emotions. Through techniques such as functional magnetic resonance imaging (fMRI) and positron emission tomography (PET), researchers have been able to pinpoint neural correlates of specific emotions, elucidating the complex interplay between brain regions and emotional processes.

By delving into the network of neural pathways involved in emotion processing, we have gained a deeper appreciation for the role of structures such as the amygdala, hippocampus, and prefrontal cortex. These regions collaborate in orchestrating emotional responses, integrating sensory information, memory, and cognitive appraisal to generate subjective feelings of fear, joy, sadness, and more. Understanding the nuanced interactions within these neural circuits has profound implications for how we perceive and manage emotions.

The influence of neurotransmitters and hormones on emotional regulation cannot be overstated. Serotonin, dopamine, norepinephrine, and oxytocin are just a few among the plethora of chemical messengers that modulate mood, arousal, and social bonding. By unraveling the delicate balance of these neurochemicals, scientists are gaining insights into the etiology of mood disorders and exploring novel pharmacological interventions for emotional disturbances.

An essential component of this integrative perspective involves acknowledging the interplay between genetics and environmental influences on emotional responses. Growing evidence suggests that genetic predispositions can interact with external factors to shape an individual's emotional repertoire and vulnerability to mental health conditions. Such findings underscore the need for personalized approaches to emotional well-being, recognizing the unique genetic and environmental determinants that contribute to an individual's emotional landscape.

In conclusion, the journey through the neurobiological underpinnings of emotional responses has not only expanded our knowledge but also underscored the interconnected nature of biological, psychological, and sociocultural factors in shaping our emotional experiences.

The Role of Context and Environment in Emotional Conditioning

1. Defining Environmental Variables in Emotional Learning:

In understanding emotional learning, it is crucial to define and delve into the different environmental factors that contribute to this process. The environment encompasses a wide array of elements, including physical surroundings, social dynamics, cultural contexts, and even technological influences. These diverse variables interact with an individual's cognitive and affective processes to shape emotional conditioning. Physical surroundings play a pivotal role in emotional learning, as they provide the backdrop against which emotional stimuli are encountered. For instance, the comfort or discomfort of a physical space can influence the intensity and valence of emotional reactions. Additionally, the presence of specific sensory cues within an environment can trigger conditioned emotional responses, further reinforcing the link between environmental stimuli and learned emotions. Social environments also wield significant sway over emotional conditioning. Interactions with peers, family members, and community members can mold emotional responses through social modeling and reinforcement mechanisms. Cultural contexts introduce another layer of complexity, as norms, values, and traditions shape the emotional landscape within a society, influencing what elicits emotional responses and how they are expressed. Moreover, technological advances have introduced new environmental variables, such as virtual environments and digital stimuli, prompting unique avenues for emotional conditioning. These novel factors underscore the multifaceted nature of environmental influences on emotional learning. Understanding and defining these environmental variables is integral to comprehensively grasping the mechanisms of emotional conditioning and its implications for individual and collective well-being.

2. Theoretical Models of Contextual Interactions:

Theoretical models play a critical role in shaping our understanding of how environmental contexts contribute to the process of emotional learning. One prominent theoretical framework is the context-dependency model, which posits that emotional responses are not only influenced by specific stimuli but are also heavily contingent on the context in which these stimuli occur. This perspective underscores the dynamic interplay between the organism and its immediate environment, emphasizing that emotional reactions are not fixed entities but are continuously shaped by the ever-changing contextual landscape. Additionally, the ecological systems theory, advanced by Urie Bronfenbrenner, offers a comprehensive framework for comprehending the multifaceted web of influences that constitute an individual's environment. This model highlights the interconnected layers of influence, from the immediate surroundings to broader societal and cultural forces, and their impact on emotional development and expression. Furthermore, the transactional model of environmental influence proposes a bidirectional relationship between the individual and the environment, emphasizing the reciprocal nature of influence wherein the individual actively shapes and is shaped by their surroundings. This model underscores the agency of the individual in co-creating their emotional experiences within specific contexts, thereby shedding light on the complex dynamics at play in emotional conditioning. The bioecological model, advocated by Gita Badiyan and Richard Lerner, extends the focus beyond immediate physical environments to encompass biological, social, and historical factors, providing a holistic lens through which to understand emotional responses in varied contexts. Moreover, the sociocultural model delves into the cultural and societal dimensions of emotional conditioning, illuminating how norms, values, and belief systems embedded within a given culture can profoundly shape emotional processes. These theoretical models collectively offer key insights into the ways in which contextual interactions exert influence on emotional conditioning, offering a robust foundation for empirical investigations and practical applications in diverse settings.

3. Impact of Social Environments on Emotional Responses:

From early developmental stages to adult experiences, the interactions within social contexts have been demonstrated to significantly influence how individuals interpret, express, and regulate emotions. Research in psychology has extensively explored the impact of social dynamics on emotional conditioning and behavioral outcomes. The web of interpersonal relationships, social norms, and cultural practices collectively contribute to the emotional landscape of individuals. The presence of supportive and nurturing social networks has been associated with enhanced emotional resilience and adaptive coping mechanisms. Conversely, exposure to social adversities, such as bullying, discrimination, or social exclusion, can engender maladaptive emotional patterns and psychological distress. Furthermore, the contagion of emotions within social groups, known as emotional contagion, underscores the interconnectedness of emotional experiences among individuals. This phenomenon underscores the reciprocal influence of emotional expressions and reactions within social circles. Additionally, the influence of influential figures, such as family members, peers, mentors, and community leaders, cannot be understated in shaping the emotional climate for individuals. Their behaviors, attitudes, and emotional displays serve as models that influence the emotional learning and regulation processes of others. Moreover, the broader societal context, encompassing cultural values, socio-economic disparities, and institutional norms, significantly shapes the emotional landscape. Cultural variations in emotional expression and regulation underscore the profound influence of social environments. Collectively, these factors contribute to the complexity of emotional responses within diverse social contexts. Understanding the impact of social environments on emotional responses is pivotal in various domains, including clinical psychology, education, organizational behavior, and public policy.

4. Role of Physical Spaces in Conditioning Processes:

The arrangement, design, and sensory attributes of these environments can serve as potent cues for associative learning and emotional regulation. Whether it is the serenity of a natural landscape or the hustle and bustle of an urban setting, physical spaces have the capacity to shape our emotional experiences in profound ways.

Consider the impact of architecture on emotional conditioning. Architectural elements such as lighting, spatial layout, and acoustics can create atmospheres that evoke specific emotional states. For instance, the soaring ceilings and elaborate ornamentation of a cathedral may instill feelings of awe and reverence, while the intimate confines of a cozy café might elicit a sense of comfort and relaxation. These environmental features can become embedded within an individual's emotional repertoire, shaping their subsequent behavioral and affective responses within similar settings.

The role of physical spaces extends beyond mere aesthetics. The functionality and utility of a space can also modulate emotional conditioning. For example, the contrast between a tranquil library and a bustling marketplace illustrates how the purpose and activity within a space can mold emotional experiences. Through repeated exposure and reinforcement, individuals develop contextualized emotional associations with distinct settings, influencing their affective states and behavioral inclinations within those environments.

The interplay between physical spaces and emotional conditioning is linked to the concept of place attachment. Humans form strong emotional bonds with specific locations, imbuing them with personal and collective significance. These attachments can contribute to the development of emotional schemas tied to certain places, amplifying the influence of the physical environment on affective responses and memories. Understanding this dynamic interplay is crucial for comprehending the complex web of factors that contribute to emotional conditioning across varied environmental contexts.

5. Cultural Nuances and Ethological Perspectives:

The interplay between cultural norms, beliefs, and practices significantly influences how individuals perceive and respond to emotionally evocative stimuli. Ethological perspectives provide a deeper understanding of the universality of certain emotional responses across different societies while also highlighting the divergences that exist due to specific cultural contexts.

Cultural variations in emotional expressions and interpretations are rooted in the distinct societal values, traditions, and communication patterns prevalent within different communities. For instance, the display rules governing the expression of emotions may vary widely across cultures, impacting the conditioning processes associated with specific emotions. Moreover, the socialization practices and familial dynamics within a cultural group can shape an individual's emotional learning experiences, contributing to diverse conditioned responses.

Ethological perspectives offer valuable insights into the evolutionary and adaptive significance of emotional conditioning in human and non-human species. By examining ethological frameworks, researchers can discern the underlying biological mechanisms that drive emotional responses and their modulation by cultural factors. This interdisciplinary approach enhances our comprehension of how cultural contexts interact with instinctual and learned emotional behaviors, enriching the field of emotional conditioning studies.

Cross-cultural research in ethology unveils the connections between cultural diversity and behavioral plasticity. It elucidates how ecological factors, such as geographical landscapes and resource availability, contribute to the development of distinct emotional repertoires across different societies. Understanding these intricacies fosters a more comprehensive grasp of emotional conditioning phenomena, transcending beyond singular cultural paradigms to encompass a global perspective.

6. Technological Advances in Context Assessment:

Advancements in technology have revolutionized the assessment of contextual factors in emotional conditioning. Traditionally, researchers relied on manual observation and subjective assessments to identify environmental stimuli influencing emotional responses. However, contemporary tools and methodologies have significantly enhanced our ability to capture and analyze contextual variables with a higher degree of precision and objectivity.

One notable innovation is the use of wearable physiological monitoring devices, such as smartwatches and biosensors, to continuously track an individual's physiological arousal and activity patterns in real time. These devices can provide invaluable data on how varying environmental contexts influence the individual's emotional states, offering insights into the dynamics of emotional conditioning within different settings.

The integration of geospatial technologies, including GPS tracking and geographic information systems (GIS), has enabled researchers to spatially map and analyze the impact of specific locations and spatial arrangements on emotional experiences. By correlating emotional responses with environmental features, such as urban landscapes, natural settings, or built environments, researchers can gain a deeper understanding of how contextual cues shape emotional learning and expression.

In addition, advancements in data analytics and machine learning algorithms have empowered researchers to process large-scale contextual datasets more efficiently. By employing sophisticated computational models, patterns and associations between contextual variables and emotional responses can be identified, contributing to a more comprehensive understanding of the complex interplay between environmental factors and emotional conditioning.

Remote sensing technologies, including video surveillance and ambient audio recording, have also been leveraged to capture subtle contextual cues that may elicit emotional responses. Ethical considerations and privacy concerns are paramount in the application of these technologies, necessitating careful adherence to ethical guidelines and informed consent procedures in research endeavors.

Virtual reality (VR) and augmented reality (AR) systems have emerged as powerful tools for simulating diverse environmental scenarios and manipulating contextual elements to study their impact on emotional states. Through immersive simulations, researchers can systematically expose individuals to controlled environmental stimuli while precisely measuring their emotional reactions, providing valuable insights into the mechanisms of contextual emotional conditioning.

7. Challenges in Isolating Contextual Factors:

Isolating contextual factors in emotional conditioning presents a formidable challenge for researchers across disciplines. The interplay between an individual's internal state and the external environment complicates the task of disentangling specific contextual influences on emotional responses. One of the primary hurdles in isolating contextual factors lies in the dynamic nature of real-world environments. Unlike controlled laboratory settings, natural contexts are characterized by a multitude of interconnected variables, making it arduous to pinpoint the precise elements that contribute to emotional conditioning. Furthermore, individuals experience context in highly subjective ways, adding another layer of complexity to the process of isolating and measuring contextual factors.

Another significant challenge in isolating contextual factors stems from the ethical considerations involved in manipulating environmental variables. While experimental control is crucial for rigorous research, ethically altering real-world contexts to study emotional conditioning raises ethical concerns about the potential impact on participants' well-being. Balancing the need for ecological validity with ethical principles poses a delicate dilemma for researchers seeking to isolate contextual factors in emotional conditioning studies.

Additionally, the multidimensionality of context further complicates isolation efforts. Context encompasses not only physical aspects such as location and sensory stimuli but also social dynamics, cultural norms, and historical backgrounds. Teasing apart the individual contributions of these diverse contextual dimensions to emotional responses requires sophisticated methodological approaches and innovative research designs. Complex statistical analyses and advanced modeling techniques may be necessary to disentangle the web of contextual factors at play.

The potential for confounding variables looms large when attempting to isolate contextual factors. External influences, such as unforeseen events or interpersonal interactions, can confound the relationship between specific contextual elements and emotional conditioning. Mitigating these confounding factors demands meticulous planning and thorough consideration of potential sources of interference, thus calling for heightened methodological rigor in studying contextual influences on emotional responses.

ADVANCED CONCEPTS - DIFFERENTIATION & GENERALIZATION

Fundamentals of Differentiation in Emotional Responses

1. Introduction:

In the sphere of emotional responses, differentiation refers to the ability to perceive and express a wide range of distinct emotions with clarity and precision. Understanding how individuals differentiate between various emotional states provides valuable insights into their cognitive and affective processes. In essence, differentiation allows individuals to not only recognize and label specific emotions but also to discern subtle nuances within similar emotional states. The role of differentiation is linked to key psychological constructs such as emotional intelligence, empathy, and self-awareness. By analyzing an individual's capacity for emotional response differentiation, researchers and practitioners gain valuable information about their adaptive functioning, interpersonal relationships, and overall well-being. Within the broader scope of psychological theories, differentiation in emotional responses aligns with various theoretical frameworks, including the psychodynamic, cognitive, and socioemotional perspectives. Psychodynamic theories emphasize the significance of emotional differentiation in the development of personality structure and the resolution of internal conflicts. Cognitive theories underscore the role of differentiation in shaping perception, memory, and decision-making processes related to emotional experiences. Additionally, socioemotional theories highlight the impact of differentiation on social interactions, communication patterns, and relational dynamics. This comprehensive exploration of differentiation in emotional responses sets the stage for a nuanced examination of its underlying mechanisms, developmental trajectories, and practical implications.

2. Emotional Response Differentiation:

Emotional response differentiation refers to the process by which individuals perceive and respond to distinct emotional stimuli with varying degrees of intensity, complexity, and specificity. In essence, it involves the ability to discriminate between different emotional experiences, recognize their unique qualities, and generate tailored affective responses. This cognitive and affective flexibility allows individuals to manage a wide range of emotionally laden situations with precision and adaptability.

At the core of emotional response differentiation lies the capacity to discern subtle nuances in emotional stimuli, leading to refined categorization and interpretation of affective states. This nuanced discrimination enables individuals to distinguish between emotions that may share common features but possess unique underlying characteristics. By accurately identifying these distinctions, individuals can modulate their emotional reactions in a more granular manner, thereby optimizing their adaptive functioning in social, interpersonal, and environmental contexts.

Emotional response differentiation encompasses the ability to regulate the intensity and duration of emotional responses based on the specific demands of a given situation. Individuals proficient in differentiating emotional responses display a heightened sensitivity to contextual cues and are adept at tailoring their affective expressions to align with situational requirements. This adaptive regulation facilitates effective emotional communication, promotes harmonious social interactions, and fosters emotional well-being.

Psychophysiological research has highlighted the role of various neural structures and mechanisms in facilitating emotional response differentiation. The interplay between limbic system regions, prefrontal cortical areas, and autonomic nervous system activity contributes to the fine-grained differentiation of emotional experiences. Furthermore, neuroimaging studies have elucidated the neural correlates associated with differential processing of discrete emotions, shedding light on the underlying neural substrates of emotion-specific differentiation processes.

3. Physiological Basis and Neural Correlates:

The differentiation of emotional responses is linked to the physiological processes and neural correlates within the human body. Understanding the underlying physiological basis provides a crucial framework for comprehending the nature of emotional response differentiation. At a fundamental level, the autonomic nervous system plays a pivotal role in the regulation and manifestation of differentiated emotional responses. This system comprises the sympathetic and parasympathetic branches, which exert influence over various bodily functions in response to emotional stimuli. The sympathetic branch, often associated with the 'fight or flight' response, triggers physiological changes such as increased heart rate, rapid breathing, and heightened arousal. In contrast, the parasympathetic branch facilitates calming and restorative processes, promoting relaxation and reduced arousal levels. These distinct physiological patterns are essential in differentiating emotional responses and contribute to the diverse array of emotional states experienced by individuals. Furthermore, advances in neuroscience have elucidated the neural substrates involved in emotional response differentiation. Research has identified key brain regions, including the amygdala, prefrontal cortex, and insula, as integral components in processing and encoding emotional experiences. The amygdala, renowned for its role in emotional processing, is central to the rapid appraisal and recognition of emotional stimuli, thereby initiating appropriate physiological and behavioral responses. Meanwhile, the prefrontal cortex exerts regulatory control over emotional reactivity and aids in the cognitive evaluation of emotional contexts, influencing the differentiation of emotional responses. Additionally, the insula contributes to the subjective awareness of bodily sensations, fostering the nuanced discrimination of emotional experiences. Moreover, neuroimaging techniques such as functional magnetic resonance imaging (fMRI) have enabled researchers to visualize the dynamic interplay among these brain regions during the experience of varied emotional states. By delineating the interconnections and functional dynamics of these neural structures, researchers have garnered valuable insights into the neural correlates of emotional response differentiation. Overall, gaining a comprehensive understanding of the physiological underpinnings and neural mechanisms associated with differentiated emotional responses illuminates the complex interplay between mind and body in traversing the tapestry of human emotions.

4. Behavioral Manifestations and Indicators:

Behavioral manifestations of emotional response differentiation are crucial indicators that reveal the nature of human behavior in response to stimuli. These behavioral manifestations encompass a wide spectrum of observable actions, including facial expressions, body language, verbal responses, and physiological changes. Understanding these behavioral indicators provides valuable insights into the complex processes underlying emotional differentiation. Facial expressions are a fundamental aspect of behavioral manifestations, as they often serve as immediate and unfiltered reflections of emotional states. The nuanced shifts in facial muscles and microexpressions can convey subtle differentiations in emotional responses, offering researchers and clinicians a window into the tapestry of human emotions. Furthermore, body language plays a pivotal role in signaling emotional nuances, with postures, gestures, and movements reflecting variations in emotional differentiation. Verbal responses also form a significant part of behavioral indicators, as the choice of words, tone of voice, and linguistic patterns can convey distinct emotional nuances. Additionally, physiological changes, such as heart rate variability, skin conductance, and other autonomic responses, provide objective measures of emotional differentiation. These multidimensional behavioral indicators not only enrich our understanding of emotional differentiation but also inform practical applications in clinical and therapeutic settings. Studying behavioral manifestations in the context of emotional differentiation requires meticulous attention to detail and the integration of diverse methodologies. Observational studies, experimental paradigms, and advanced technology-based assessments offer valuable approaches to capture and analyze behavioral indicators with precision and depth. Integrating subjective self-reports with objective observations further enriches the assessment of emotional differentiation, providing comprehensive insights into the complexity of human emotional experiences. Moreover, understanding the influence of contextual variables on behavioral manifestations is essential for interpreting emotional responses accurately. Environmental factors, social dynamics, cultural norms, and situational contexts all contribute to shaping behavioral indicators of emotional differentiation. Considering individual differences and personality traits adds another layer of complexity to the interpretation of behavioral manifestations.

5. Experimental Approaches and Methodologies:

Experimental approaches and methodologies play a vital role in elucidating the complexities of emotional response differentiation. These approaches are designed to systematically investigate and analyze the various components, factors, and mechanisms underlying the differentiation of emotional responses. Researchers employ a wide array of experimental methods to probe into this phenomenon. One commonly used methodology involves the use of well-structured laboratory experiments where participants are exposed to carefully designed stimuli aimed at eliciting specific emotional responses. These stimuli can range from visual images and auditory cues to more immersive virtual reality experiences, allowing for controlled yet ecologically valid investigations. Additionally, physiological measures such as heart rate variability, skin conductance, and neuroimaging techniques are often integrated to provide a comprehensive understanding of the underlying neural and physiological processes associated with differentiated emotional responses. Furthermore, longitudinal and cross-sectional studies are employed to track the developmental trajectories and stability of emotional response differentiation across different populations and age groups. Advanced statistical analyses, including multivariate approaches and machine learning algorithms, are utilized to disentangle complex patterns and relationships within the datasets acquired from experimental studies. Importantly, interdisciplinary collaborations between psychologists, neuroscientists, and technologists have led to the development of innovative methodologies that combine behavioral assessments with cutting-edge technological advancements, thereby offering new insights into emotional response differentiation. This iterative process of refining and updating experimental approaches and methodologies is essential to ensure the rigorous investigation and understanding of differentiated emotional responses, laying the groundwork for future advancements in this field.

6. Influence of Contextual Variables:

The influence of contextual variables on emotional response differentiation is a complex and multifaceted area of study within the field of emotional conditioning. Contextual variables encompass a wide range of environmental and situational factors that can modulate an individual's emotional experiences and expressions. These variables can include but are not limited to social cues, cultural norms, physical settings, and temporal dynamics. Understanding how contextual variables shape emotional responses is essential for comprehensively elucidating the complexities of human behavior and emotion. One key aspect of contextual variables is their role in mediating the appraisal of emotional stimuli. The context in which an emotional stimulus is encountered can significantly impact the interpretation and evaluation of the stimulus, subsequently influencing the intensity and valence of the emotional response. For instance, the same facial expression displayed in different social contexts may elicit distinct emotional reactions, highlighting the importance of context in shaping emotional differentiation. Furthermore, contextual variables can also act as moderators of emotional expression. Social norms and situational demands govern the acceptability and appropriateness of certain emotional displays, leading individuals to modulate their emotional responses based on the prevailing contextual cues. Additionally, contextual factors can interact with an individual's cognitive processes and emotional regulation strategies, further shaping the differentiation of emotional responses. Cultural variations in emotional display rules and norms provide compelling evidence for the profound impact of contextual variables on emotional responsiveness. Moreover, the temporal dimension of contextual variables should not be overlooked. Emotions experienced in a specific temporal context may differ from those experienced in another time frame, emphasizing the dynamic nature of contextual influences on emotional differentiation. Understanding the interplay between contextual variables and emotional responses holds substantial implications across various domains, including clinical psychology, interpersonal relationships, and organizational behavior.

7. Role of Individual Differences and Personality:

Individual differences encompass a wide array of characteristics, including but not limited to traits, preferences, beliefs, values, and cognitive styles, all of which can significantly influence an individual's emotional responses to various stimuli. Personality, as a complex and multifaceted construct, further shapes how individuals perceive, interpret, and express emotions, thereby impacting their differential responses.

One of the key factors influencing emotional response differentiation is the individual's temperament, which constitutes their innate emotional and behavioral tendencies. Research has indicated that individuals with different temperamental profiles may exhibit varying degrees of sensitivity, reactivity, and adaptability to emotional stimuli, consequently leading to diverse patterns of differentiation in their emotional responses. Moreover, certain personality traits, such as neuroticism, extraversion, openness, conscientiousness, and agreeableness, have been linked to distinct patterns of emotional response differentiation. For instance, individuals high in neuroticism may display heightened emotional reactivity and lower levels of differentiation, while those high in conscientiousness might exhibit more regulated and differentiated emotional responses.

Additionally, the influence of cognitive processes on emotional response differentiation cannot be overlooked. Variations in cognitive styles, information processing mechanisms, and attentional biases contribute to individual differences in perceiving, evaluating, and modulating emotional experiences. Furthermore, cultural and familial contexts play a pivotal role in shaping an individual's attitudes towards emotions, their regulation strategies, and their expressive behaviors, thus interfacing with their level of differentiation in emotional responses.

The implications of individual differences and personality traits for emotional response differentiation extend beyond theoretical constructs to practical contexts such as clinical interventions, psychotherapy, and educational settings. Tailoring therapeutic approaches based on an individual's unique personality profile and emotional differentiation patterns holds promise for enhancing treatment outcomes and promoting emotional well-being. Similarly, understanding these factors in educational contexts can help educators design personalized learning experiences that consider students' diverse emotional responsiveness, thus fostering a conducive and inclusive academic environment.

8. Integration with Watson's Original Concepts:

The integration of differentiation in emotional responses with Watson's original concepts presents a significant advancement in understanding the nuances and intricacies of emotional conditioning. Building upon Watson's foundational work, the incorporation of the concept of differentiation provides a more comprehensive framework for examining how emotional stimuli elicit varied responses among individuals. By integrating this aspect, we can delve deeper into the complexity of emotional reactions, shedding light on the diverse range of responses observed in real-world scenarios. This integration serves to enrich our understanding of emotional conditioning processes and their implications for psychological theory and clinical practice. When viewed through the lens of Watson's original principles, the role of differentiation becomes evident in elucidating the heterogeneity of emotional responses within the context of stimulus generalization. By acknowledging the individualized nature of emotional experiences, this integration enhances the applicability and relevance of Watson's theories in contemporary research and practical settings. Furthermore, aligning differentiation with Watson's original concepts fosters a more holistic perspective on emotional conditioning, emphasizing the multifaceted nature of human emotional responses. This integration also underscores the dynamic interplay between environmental cues, emotional stimuli, and learned associations—a key aspect of Watson's theoretical framework. Moreover, by integrating differentiation, we bridge the gap between basic conditioning principles and the manifestations of emotional responses in varied contexts. This synthesis opens doors for exploring new dimensions of emotional conditioning, paving the way for innovative research approaches and refined therapeutic interventions. Through this integration, Watson's original concepts are revitalized and enriched, offering a renewed understanding of emotional conditioning phenomena that accounts for the diverse and nuanced nature of human emotions. As we continue to explore the synergies between differentiation and Watson's original theories, we uncover a wealth of insights that deepen our comprehension of emotional conditioning processes and their far-reaching implications. This integration not only honors Watson's contributions to the field but also propels his theories into the forefront of contemporary discourse on emotional responses and behavior.

9. Implications for Further Research:

The integration of differentiation in emotional responses with Watson's original concepts opens a promising avenue for future investigations. One crucial area of future inquiry lies in unraveling the neurobiological underpinnings of differentiated emotional responses. Exploring the neural correlates and physiological mechanisms associated with differentiating emotional stimuli can provide valuable insights into the processes underlying emotional conditioning. Moreover, the exploration of how contextual variables interact with differentiation in emotional responses represents a fertile ground for future studies. Investigating the influence of situational contexts on the process of differentiation and its impact on emotional reactivity holds potential for advancing our comprehension of emotional conditioning. Furthermore, delving into the role of individual differences and personality traits in modulating differentiated emotional responses offers an intriguing path for future research. Understanding how personality dimensions shape the ability to differentiate emotional stimuli can significantly contribute to tailoring interventions and treatments in clinical settings. Additionally, embracing diverse experimental approaches and methodologies, such as advanced imaging techniques and behavior-based assessments, can enrich our comprehension of differentiated emotional responses. The utilization of multi-modal methodologies enables a comprehensive investigation of the complex interplay between psychological, physiological, and environmental factors in shaping emotional differentiation. Moreover, future research endeavors should seek to elucidate the practical implications of differentiated emotional responses in real-world scenarios. Employing case examples and ecological momentary assessment methods could shed light on how differentiated emotional responses manifest in naturalistic settings and their significance in influencing behavior and decision-making. Finally, exploring the cross-cultural manifestations of emotional differentiation presents a captivating avenue for future investigations. Examining how cultural norms and values influence the process of differentiation and generalization in emotional conditioning can yield valuable insights into the universality or cultural specificity of these phenomena. Overall, addressing these directions for future research has the potential to deepen our understanding of emotional conditioning and expand the applicability of differentiation in diverse domains, ranging from clinical psychology to social and organizational contexts.

Mechanisms of Generalization in Emotional Conditioning

1. Theoretical Foundations:

Generalization mechanisms encompass the broad spectrum of psychological responses and behavioral adaptations that extend beyond the specific stimuli initially associated with an emotional experience. At its core, generalization posits that conditioned responses to a specific stimulus broaden to encompass similar stimuli, thus revealing the underlying complexity of human emotional processing. The theoretical frameworks underpinning this phenomenon draw from diverse disciplines, including behaviorism, cognitive psychology, and neuroscience. A central tenet of these foundations is the principle of stimulus generalization, which asserts that organisms generalize their learned responses to novel stimuli that share perceptual features with the original conditioned stimulus. This process is guided by the perceptual similarity between the original and novel stimuli, offering profound insights into the mechanisms governing emotional learning. Additionally, the integration of cognitive theories underscores the role of mental representations and categorization processes in shaping the extent and scope of generalization. Importantly, the theoretical landscape also encompasses discussions on the impact of contextual factors and situational cues on the generalization process. Examining the interplay between these varied theoretical perspectives unveils the multifaceted nature of generalization and its implications for understanding human emotional reactivity. Moreover, advances in neuroscientific research have further elucidated the neural substrates associated with generalization, shedding light on the interplay between cognitive and affective processes.

2. Comparison with Differentiation:

While generalization involves the extension of conditioned responses to stimuli resembling the original conditioned stimulus, differentiation refers to the ability to discriminate between similar but distinct stimuli to elicit specific responses. A key distinction between generalization and differentiation lies in their respective roles in the formation and modulation of emotional responses. Generalization, rooted in the adaptive nature of conditioning, allows for the broadening of conditioned responses to ensure the transfer of learned associations to novel stimuli with shared characteristics. On the other hand, differentiation serves as a safeguard against indiscriminate response elicitation, enabling organisms to discern meaningful differences among stimuli and respond selectively.

The comparative analysis further underscores the dynamic nature of generalization and differentiation in shaping emotional conditioning. While generalization facilitates the efficient transfer of learned responses across stimuli variants, differentiation acts as a regulatory mechanism to prevent overgeneralization and promote nuanced discrimination. Understanding this delicate balance is crucial in unraveling the complexities of emotional processing and behavior.

Examining the interrelation between generalization and differentiation sheds light on their implications for clinical applications. Effective therapeutic interventions necessitate a comprehensive comprehension of how these mechanisms interact and influence emotional responses in various contexts. By delineating the dynamics between generalization and differentiation, practitioners can tailor treatment approaches to optimize emotional learning and mitigate maladaptive responses.

Additionally, insights from the comparative analysis offer valuable implications for experimental design and research methodologies in the field of emotional conditioning. By carefully considering the interplay between generalization and differentiation, researchers can refine paradigms to elucidate the nuances of emotional learning and behavior. Moreover, recognizing the reciprocal influence between these mechanisms paves the way for innovative investigations that address gaps in current understanding and propel the field forward.

3. Neural Pathways and Physiological Underpinnings:

The processes underlying emotional conditioning and generalization are closely intertwined with the neurobiological and physiological mechanisms within the human brain. Within the sphere of emotional conditioning, neural pathways play a pivotal role in shaping and perpetuating learned responses. Specifically, the amygdala, an almond-shaped cluster of nuclei located within the temporal lobe, is often regarded as a central hub for processing emotional stimuli. Studies have consistently shown that the amygdala is implicated in both the acquisition and expression of conditioned fear responses, highlighting its significance in emotional learning. Moreover, the interplay between the amygdala and other regions such as the prefrontal cortex further modulates the complex array of emotional responses observed in individuals.

Understanding the physiological underpinnings of emotional conditioning entails delving into the interplay of neurotransmitters and hormones. For instance, the release of neurotransmitters like dopamine, serotonin, and norepinephrine has been linked to the consolidation and retrieval of emotionally charged memories, thereby influencing the process of generalization. Additionally, the endocrine system exerts its influence through the release of stress-related hormones such as cortisol, which can potentiate the encoding of emotional experiences and subsequent generalization across stimuli.

In the context of generalization, the dynamic interactions within neural circuits contribute significantly to the transfer of learned responses across similar environmental cues. Research has elucidated the phenomenon of neural plasticity, wherein the connectivity and strength of synaptic pathways are dynamically altered in response to environmental input. This neuroplasticity serves as the foundation for the generalization of emotional responses, as the brain integrates disparate sensory information to form associative networks that facilitate the extension of conditioned emotional responses to stimuli resembling the original conditioned cue.

Recent advancements in neuroscience have shed light on the role of neuroimaging techniques in unraveling the neural substrates of generalized emotional responses. Functional magnetic resonance imaging (fMRI) studies have provided valuable insights into the activation patterns of various brain regions during generalized emotional processing, offering empirical evidence to substantiate theoretical frameworks. Such research endeavors are instrumental in delineating the specific neural correlates associated with the generalization of emotional conditioning, thereby enriching our comprehension of the underlying neural pathways and physiological dynamics governing this phenomenon.

4. Role of Environmental Cues in Generalization:

Generalization in emotional conditioning involves the extension of learned responses to stimuli that are similar to the conditioned stimulus (CS). One significant aspect contributing to generalization is the role of environmental cues. Environmental cues encompass a broad range of sensory inputs, including visual, auditory, olfactory, and tactile stimuli, that may resemble or share certain characteristics with the original CS. These cues play a pivotal role in shaping the generalization process and can impact the strength and specificity of conditioned responses. Understanding the relationship between environmental cues and generalization is crucial in elucidating the complexities of emotional conditioning. For instance, in a classic experiment involving Pavlovian conditioning, the presence of specific contextual cues, such as the location where the conditioning took place or the background noise present during the conditioning, significantly influenced the extent of generalization of the conditioned response. Moreover, studies have shown that environmental contexts rich in familiar cues can promote more robust generalization compared to novel or ambiguous environments. This highlights the significance of environmental familiarity and its influence on the generalization of emotional responses. Furthermore, the role of environmental cues in generalization has practical implications in various domains, including clinical psychology and behavioral interventions. Therapeutic settings often leverage environmental cues to facilitate the transfer of learned coping mechanisms and emotional regulation strategies from structured therapy sessions to real-life contexts. By strategically incorporating relevant environmental cues into the therapeutic environment, clinicians can enhance the generalization of adaptive emotional responses beyond the clinical setting. Additionally, the examination of environmental cue-based generalization provides valuable insights into the underlying processes of associative learning and memory consolidation. It sheds light on how environmental features become integrated into the neural representations of learned emotional associations, thus influencing the breadth and precision of generalization.

5. Factors Influencing the Extent of Generalization:

Generalization in emotional conditioning is not a uniform process and can be influenced by various factors that shape the extent and scope of generalization. One crucial factor is the similarity between the conditioned stimulus (CS) and the stimuli present during the conditioning phase. Research has shown that the more similar the CS is to other stimuli encountered in the environment, the greater the likelihood of generalization. This principle is consistent with the concept of stimulus generalization and underlines the impact of perceptual similarity on the generalization process. Additionally, the temporal proximity between the conditioned stimulus and the unconditioned stimulus (US) can affect generalization. Closer temporal contiguity may lead to broader generalization as the association between the CS and US becomes more salient, resulting in a wider spectrum of stimuli eliciting similar emotional responses. Moreover, the context in which the conditioning occurs plays a significant role in determining the extent of generalization. A change in context during the conditioning phase or subsequent testing can inhibit generalization, while a consistent context facilitates it. Furthermore, individual differences in cognitive processes, such as attention and memory, can modulate the degree of generalization. For instance, individuals with heightened attentional biases towards certain stimuli may exhibit more pronounced generalization effects. The emotional valence of the conditioned stimuli also influences generalization. Stimuli associated with strong emotional valence are more likely to lead to broad generalization compared to neutral or weakly valenced stimuli. Additionally, the presence of multiple overlapping conditioned stimuli can amplify generalization, as the cumulative effect of similar associations expands the range of stimuli eliciting comparable emotional responses. These factors collectively underscore the interplay of cognitive, perceptual, and contextual elements in shaping the extent of generalization in emotional conditioning.

6. Generalization Across Developmental Stages:

Generalization in emotional conditioning is a complex phenomenon that manifests differently across various developmental stages. During infancy and early childhood, the process of generalization is influenced by the rapid neurobiological and cognitive development occurring during this period. Infants demonstrate a tendency to generalize emotional responses to similar stimuli as they begin to differentiate between various environmental cues. This early stage lays the groundwork for subsequent generalization processes, shaping an individual's emotional responses in later years.

As children enter middle childhood and adolescence, their capacity for generalization undergoes further refinement. Cognitive abilities such as abstract reasoning and perspective-taking expand, leading to more sophisticated forms of generalization. Adolescents begin to apply learned emotional responses to diverse contexts, demonstrating an increased propensity to generalize emotional stimuli based on conceptual rather than perceptual similarities. This developmental period marks a significant shift in the scope and complexity of generalization, as individuals regulate the interplay between internal emotional states and external stimuli.

In adulthood, the process of generalization reflects cumulative experiences and learned associations. The nuanced interplay between cognitive appraisal and emotional expression shapes the generalization of emotional responses among adults. The ability to modulate and generalize emotions across different situations becomes integral to adaptive functioning in personal, social, and professional domains. Moreover, individual variations in generalization tendencies become more pronounced, influenced by factors such as personality traits, cultural background, and life experiences.

7. Implications for Therapeutic Interventions:

Understanding how emotional responses generalize to stimuli allows therapists to design more effective treatment strategies for individuals with various psychological disorders. By leveraging the principles of generalization, therapists can tailor exposure therapies to target specific triggers and enhance the effectiveness of desensitization techniques. Moreover, insights into generalization mechanisms enable clinicians to address the transfer of emotional responses across different contexts and situations. This understanding is vital in developing comprehensive intervention plans that aim to promote emotional regulation and resilience in patients. Additionally, knowledge of generalization aids in the identification of potential triggers and associated responses, facilitating the development of personalized coping strategies and emotion management techniques. Furthermore, an awareness of factors influencing the extent of generalization assists therapists in fine-tuning interventions to optimize outcomes for each individual. When applied within a therapeutic framework, an understanding of generalization mechanisms can enhance the precision and efficacy of cognitive-behavioral interventions, contributing to improved treatment outcomes and long-term symptom management. Overall, the implications of generalization mechanisms for therapeutic interventions underscore the importance of integrating empirical research on emotional conditioning into clinical practice, with the potential to significantly enhance the quality of care provided to individuals struggling with emotional dysregulation and related mental health challenges.

Experimental Evidence Supporting Watson's Principles

1. Methodological Approaches - Design and Execution:

The design phase of an experiment is characterized by the careful selection of variables, including the stimuli to be presented, the environment in which the experiment will take place, and the participants or subjects involved. The process involves defining the research question clearly and identifying the specific hypotheses that will guide the study. The selection of appropriate experimental groups and control groups is imperative in addressing confounding variables and establishing causality in emotional response patterns.

Execution of the experimental design demands scrupulous attention to detail and adherence to standardized procedures. Ethical considerations must be paramount in safeguarding the well-being of participants, whether humans or animals. Informed consent, confidentiality, and humane treatment are fundamental ethical prerequisites in executing experimental methodologies. Additionally, the precise implementation of stimulus presentations, data collection protocols, and calibration of measurement instruments are key elements in ensuring the integrity and accuracy of the results.

The meticulous recording and documentation of procedural details are critical for reproducibility and transparency in scientific inquiry. This entails comprehensive data management and systematic logging of experimental observations and measurements. Rigorous quality control measures are essential in mitigating sources of error and bias, thereby enhancing the robustness of the findings.

Validating the reliability of the chosen methodological approaches is vital in establishing the credibility and validity of the experimental outcomes. Statistical analyses, inter-rater reliability assessments, and triangulation of data from multiple sources contribute to the comprehensive validation of the methodology employed. Additionally, peer review and replication studies further consolidate the robustness and generalizability of the findings.

2. Pioneering Studies - Watson's Foundational Work:

John B. Watson's seminal studies, particularly his work with Little Albert, not only provided empirical evidence for the principles of emotional conditioning but also opened new avenues for exploring the complexities of human behavior and emotion. Watson's approach to experimental design and execution represented a significant departure from the prevailing introspective methods of his time. By employing rigorous behavioral observation and systematic manipulation of stimuli, he established a methodological framework that emphasized objectivity and quantifiability in psychological research. The precision and detail with which he documented the process of conditioning Little Albert set a new standard for experimental rigor in the discipline and continues to serve as a model for contemporary researchers.

Watson's foundational work extended beyond the laboratory setting, as he sought to apply his findings to practical domains such as advertising and education. His endeavors in these areas underscored the broad impact of his research on society, demonstrating the far-reaching implications of understanding emotional conditioning. Furthermore, his emphasis on environmental influences over innate factors challenged prevailing views on the determinants of behavior, sparking ongoing debate and shaping subsequent theoretical developments.

3. Replication and Validation of Experimental Findings:

Building upon Watson's foundational work, contemporary scholars and researchers have diligently sought to replicate and validate the empirical evidence supporting the principles of emotional conditioning. This rigorous process involves the meticulous duplication of experimental procedures and the subsequent verification of obtained results. By adhering to stringent methodological standards, scientists aim to reinforce the robustness and generalizability of Watson's theories in diverse contexts and populations.

Numerous seminal studies have successfully replicated the core principles of emotional conditioning originally expounded by Watson. These replication efforts have underscored the stability and consistency of conditioned emotional responses across various stimuli and settings. Moreover, the process of validation entails the scrutiny of experimental outcomes through peer review, statistical analyses, and cross-disciplinary collaborations. Through this multi-faceted evaluation, the validity and reliability of observed responses are rigorously scrutinized, contributing to the establishment of a strong evidential foundation for emotional conditioning phenomena.

The significance of replication and validation extends beyond mere confirmation of prior findings; it serves as a mechanism for refinement and advancement of theoretical frameworks. As researchers replicate and validate experimental results, they uncover nuances and variations that enrich our understanding of emotional conditioning processes. These insights open avenues for refining existing models and conceptualizing new paradigms that can comprehensively account for the intricacies of emotional conditioning. Notably, the integration of advanced neuroimaging techniques and psychophysiological measures has bolstered the validation process, offering nuanced insights into the neural substrates and physiological signatures of conditioned emotional responses.

4. Quantitative Analysis of Conditioned Responses:

Researchers utilize various metrics to gauge the intensity, frequency, and duration of conditioned responses across diverse stimuli. By employing rigorous statistical analyses, scholars delineate the patterns of response acquisition, extinction, and reinstatement, allowing for a comprehensive understanding of the nuances inherent in emotional conditioning. Moreover, sophisticated measurement tools such as psychophysiological indices, neuroimaging techniques, and behavioral measures enable the precise quantification of emotional reactions, providing valuable insights into the underlying mechanisms of conditioned responses. Furthermore, advances in computational modeling have facilitated the development of sophisticated algorithms for analyzing large-scale datasets, thereby enriching our comprehension of the dynamic nature of conditioned emotional responses. Ultimately, a comprehensive quantitative analysis of conditioned responses not only enhances the empirical validity of emotional conditioning theories but also furnishes a foundation for developing targeted interventions in clinical and therapeutic contexts.

5. Qualitative Insights into Emotional Reactions:

While quantitative measures provide valuable numerical data about the strength and frequency of conditioned responses, qualitative assessments offer a deeper understanding of the nuances and subjective experiences associated with emotional reactions. In the sphere of emotional conditioning, qualitative insights serve as a bridge between observable behaviors and the underlying psychological processes.

Qualitative insights into emotional reactions encompass a spectrum of perceptual, cognitive, and affective components that contribute to the holistic experience of an individual. Through qualitative analysis, researchers can capture the subtleties of emotional nuances such as apprehension, aversion, or anticipation that may not be fully captured by quantitative metrics alone. This approach allows for a more comprehensive understanding of how conditioned stimuli elicit multifaceted emotional states and shape behavioral responses.

Qualitative inquiries provide a platform for individuals to articulate their emotional experiences in their own words, enabling a more nuanced comprehension of the subjective nature of emotional reactions. By integrating qualitative narratives and personal accounts, researchers can elucidate the idiosyncratic elements of emotional conditioning, unveiling the diverse ways in which individuals interpret and respond to emotionally charged stimuli.

An essential aspect of qualitative insights lies in the exploration of contextual influences on emotional reactions. By examining environmental cues, situational factors, and cognitive appraisals, researchers can gain insight into the contextual determinants that modulate the manifestation of conditioned emotional responses. This multifaceted approach acknowledges the dynamic interplay between external triggers and internal processing, providing a comprehensive portrayal of the dynamics involved in emotional reactions.

Qualitative analysis offers a means to explore the temporal evolution of emotional reactions over time, uncovering the adaptive processes and potential shifts in response patterns. Delving into the unfolding narrative of emotional experiences enables researchers to capture the evolving nature of conditioned responses, offering invaluable insight into the resilience and adaptability of emotional conditioning over extended periods.

6. Comparative Studies on Animal and Human Subjects:

Comparative studies on animal and human subjects have yielded invaluable insights into the fundamental mechanisms of emotional responses and the extent to which they may be generalized across different organisms.

One area of focus in comparative studies has been the examination of primal emotional reactions in both animals and humans. Research has indicated that certain emotions, such as fear and aversion, are deeply rooted in evolutionary history and can be observed across diverse species. By comparing the behavioral, physiological, and neural responses to similar conditioning paradigms, scientists have gained a deeper understanding of the shared biological underpinnings of emotional reactions.

Comparative studies have facilitated the assessment of the impact of cognitive and cultural factors on emotional conditioning. While animal subjects may predominantly exhibit innate or instinctual responses to conditioned stimuli, human subjects often demonstrate more complex emotional dynamics influenced by cognition, language, and social learning. This contrast not only sheds light on the adaptive significance of emotional conditioning but also underscores the interplay between genetic predispositions and environmental influences.

The ethical implications of emotional conditioning research in both animal and human subjects have been thoroughly examined in comparative studies. Discussions surrounding the welfare of animal subjects involved in experiments, implementation of humane practices, and extrapolation of findings to human psychology have spurred critical reflections within the scientific community and shaped guidelines for ethical research practices.

Additionally, advancements in technology have enabled comparative studies to delve into the neurobiological substrates of emotional responses across species. Neuroimaging techniques and neurophysiological assessments have provided a means to compare the neural circuitry underlying emotional conditioning, offering compelling evidence of conserved neural pathways and mechanisms across diverse organisms.

7. Emerging Technologies in Emotional Response Measurement:

In recent years, the advancements in technology have significantly transformed the field of emotional response measurement. Traditional methods of assessing emotional reactions relied heavily on subjective self-report measures, which often presented limitations due to individual differences and cognitive biases. The emergence of innovative technologies has provided researchers with new tools for capturing and quantifying emotional responses with greater precision and objectivity.

One of the prominent technologies that has revolutionized emotional response measurement is functional magnetic resonance imaging (fMRI). By monitoring changes in blood flow and oxygen levels in the brain, fMRI enables researchers to identify neural correlates of specific emotions and track the activation of different brain regions in response to various stimuli. This non-invasive neuroimaging technique offers valuable insights into the underlying neural mechanisms associated with emotional processing, paving the way for a deeper understanding of emotional conditioning and its implications for psychological interventions.

Another cutting-edge technology that has garnered considerable attention in the sphere of emotional response measurement is facial expression analysis. With the aid of high-speed cameras and sophisticated algorithms, researchers can analyze micro expressions, subtle facial movements, and physiological changes such as skin conductance to gauge individuals' emotional states accurately. This objective approach to assessing emotions transcends language barriers and provides a more comprehensive understanding of emotional experiences across diverse populations.

Wearable biosensors have emerged as a groundbreaking tool for real-time monitoring of physiological markers closely linked to emotional arousal. These compact and unobtrusive devices can capture data on parameters like heart rate variability, electrodermal activity, and skin temperature, offering valuable insights into the temporal dynamics of emotional responses in naturalistic settings. The integration of wearable biosensors with machine learning algorithms also holds promise for developing personalized emotion recognition systems, catering to individual differences in emotional expression and regulation.

In addition to these technological innovations, virtual reality (VR) has created immersive environments that evoke realistic emotional responses in controlled settings. By simulating scenarios that elicit specific emotions, VR platforms provide researchers with a powerful tool for studying emotional reactivity and behavioral patterns in ecologically valid contexts. Moreover, the combination of VR with physiological monitoring devices allows for a multidimensional assessment of emotional experiences, enhancing the ecological validity of experimental protocols and enriching the understanding of emotional conditioning in complex, dynamic environments.

As these emerging technologies continue to evolve and converge, they hold immense potential for advancing our knowledge of emotional response measurement. Their interdisciplinary applications in psychology, neuroscience, and human-computer interaction open new frontiers for investigating the intricacies of emotional conditioning, individual differences in emotional processing, and the development of targeted therapeutic interventions for emotional disorders.

8. Synthesis of Experimental Data with Theoretical Models:

In the pursuit of understanding human emotional conditioning, the synthesis of experimental data with theoretical models stands as a pivotal endeavor. This process involves comprehensive integration of empirical evidence gleaned through various studies with the established theoretical frameworks within psychology and behavioral sciences. Through this synthesis, researchers aim to elucidate the underlying mechanisms and principles that govern the process of emotional conditioning and its implications for human behavior. At the core of this endeavor lies the endeavor to validate and refine existing theoretical models based on the empirical findings derived from carefully designed experiments. By harmonizing experimental results with theoretical constructs, scholars can effectively bridge the gap between abstract conceptualizations and real-world manifestations of emotional responses. Achieving this synergy is instrumental in advancing our comprehension of emotional conditioning processes, thereby paving the way for the development of more accurate and comprehensive theoretical models. Furthermore, the synthesis of experimental data with theoretical models serves to provide a deeper understanding of the nuances and complexities inherent in emotional conditioning. Researchers must traverse an extensive array of experimental data encompassing diverse variables and contexts, integrating these multifaceted insights into coherent theoretical models that capture the intricacies of emotional response dynamics. This process demands meticulous scrutiny of the empirical evidence, identification of common patterns and divergences, and the formulation of theoretical frameworks that can robustly account for the observed phenomena. Moreover, the synthesis of experimental data with theoretical models facilitates the identification of gaps in current knowledge and the establishment of avenues for future research. By critically examining the alignment between empirical findings and theoretical predictions, researchers can pinpoint areas of discrepancy or uncertainty, thereby delineating new directions for investigations and refining the theoretical underpinnings of emotional conditioning. As such, this integrative process not only consolidates the current state of knowledge but also propels the evolution of theoretical models and paradigms, fostering intellectual growth and innovation. Ultimately, the synthesis of experimental data with theoretical models represents a cornerstone in advancing our understanding of emotional conditioning, offering a scholarly roadmap for exploring the complexities of human emotions and behavior.

Applications of Differentiation and Generalization in Clinical Settings

1. Behavioral Therapy Techniques Rooted in Watsonian Theory:

Central to the application of Watson's principles is the utilization of behavioral analysis to address maladaptive patterns of behavior and emotional responses. By identifying the antecedents and consequences of behaviors, therapists can develop targeted interventions that align with Watson's emphasis on observable and measurable phenomena. One such technique is systematic desensitization, which applies the principles of differentiation and generalization to alleviate anxiety and phobias through graduated exposure. Through carefully constructed hierarchies of anxiety-inducing stimuli, individuals are guided to confront their fears while employing relaxation strategies to counteract distress. This approach exemplifies the integration of Watson's theories into a practical and effective therapeutic modality. In addition, operant conditioning techniques, such as token economies, reinforce adaptive behaviors through the consistent application of rewards, thereby promoting sustainable change. These strategies form the cornerstone of cognitive-behavioral therapies, wherein the restructuring of maladaptive thought patterns is coupled with behavior modification rooted in Watsonian principles. Furthermore, contingency management interventions, which manipulate environmental triggers to shape desired behaviors, directly draw upon Watson's notions of stimulus-response relationships. By cultivating an understanding of how stimuli evoke emotional reactions and subsequent behaviors, clinicians can tailor interventions to foster adaptive responses. The incorporation of these techniques into clinical contexts reflects the relevance of Watson's contributions to the field of psychology, positioning his principles as indispensable tools for promoting emotional well-being and behavioral change.

2. Role of Differentiation in Anxiety Treatment:

Anxiety disorders are among the most prevalent mental health conditions, posing significant challenges to individuals' daily functioning and overall well-being. In the context of Watsonian theory, the role of differentiation in anxiety treatment is paramount. Differentiation, which involves discriminating between various stimuli and responses, holds crucial significance in understanding and addressing anxiety-related concerns.

In the sphere of anxiety treatment, differentiation plays a pivotal role in helping individuals recognize and discern the triggers or cues that elicit anxious responses. By fostering an understanding of distinct stimuli and their associated emotional reactions, clinicians can assist clients in gaining insight into the specific sources of their anxiety. Through targeted interventions, individuals can learn to differentiate between rational and irrational fears, thereby empowering them to confront their anxieties in a systematic manner. Moreover, the process of differentiation enables clients to identify maladaptive thought patterns and behavioral responses, laying the groundwork for effective intervention strategies.

The incorporation of differentiation techniques within cognitive-behavioral therapy (CBT) offers a promising avenue for addressing anxiety-related symptoms. CBT interventions leverage differentiation as a means of challenging distorted cognitive processes and modifying dysfunctional behavioral patterns. By guiding individuals to differentiate between genuine threats and perceived dangers, therapists can facilitate the development of adaptive coping mechanisms and stress management skills. Through this approach, clients can gradually reframe their interpretations of anxiety-provoking situations, leading to reduced distress and enhanced emotional regulation.

Additionally, differentiation holds implications for exposure-based therapies, such as systematic desensitization, where individuals progressively confront feared stimuli while discerning between safe and threatening cues. This process of discrimination fosters gradual habituation and diminishes the exaggerated fear response characteristic of anxiety disorders. By refining their ability to differentiate between harmless stimuli and genuine threats, clients can experience a sense of mastery over their anxiety, ultimately paving the way for enduring symptom relief.

It is essential to underscore the need for tailored differentiation-based interventions that align with the diverse manifestations of anxiety. While some individuals may struggle with specific phobic triggers, others may contend with generalized anxiety or panic-related concerns. Therapeutic approaches must be attuned to each individual's unique experiences and perceptual nuances, ensuring that differentiation strategies accurately address their specific anxiety presentations. Acknowledging the multifaceted nature of anxiety underscores the importance of personalized and differentiated interventions that cater to the nuanced needs of each client.

3. Generalization Approaches in Phobia Management:

Phobias, often characterized by intense and irrational fears, can significantly impact an individual's quality of life. When addressing phobias in clinical settings, understanding the principles of generalization is crucial for devising effective therapeutic interventions. Generalization refers to the process by which a learned response broadens to additional stimuli that share similarities with the original conditioned stimulus. In the context of phobia management, generalization approaches play a pivotal role in helping individuals overcome irrational fears and associated avoidance behaviors.

One commonly employed strategy involves systematic desensitization, a behavioral technique rooted in the principles of generalization. This approach gradually exposes individuals to feared stimuli or situations while simultaneously teaching relaxation techniques to counteract anxiety responses. By systematically introducing stimuli of increasing similarity to the feared object or situation, clients can learn to generalize feelings of calm and control across a broader range of triggers. Through this process, the client experiences a shift from fear and avoidance to a sense of mastery and adaptability.

Closely related to systematic desensitization is the concept of stimulus generalization. This principle recognizes that individuals may exhibit fear responses not only to the specific phobic stimulus but also to stimuli resembling the feared object. Therapists employ strategies to encourage the transfer of adaptive responses from the treated stimulus to related stimuli, promoting a more comprehensive reduction in phobic reactions.

Another vital aspect of generalization in phobia management is the consideration of context and environmental cues. Clients may initially respond positively within the therapist's office but struggle to generalize these responses to real-world settings. To address this, therapists use cognitive restructuring techniques to help clients recognize and challenge irrational thoughts that impede generalization. By fostering awareness of the transferability of coping strategies across diverse settings, individuals can enhance their capacity to confront phobic triggers beyond the therapy environment.

Virtual reality exposure therapy represents an innovative application of generalization principles in phobia management. By simulating anxiety-inducing scenarios in a controlled and adjustable virtual environment, this approach facilitates the generalization of adaptive responses to various real-life situations. The immersive nature of virtual reality allows for repeated exposure to feared stimuli, promoting generalization across a spectrum of relevant contexts.

4. Implications for Cognitive-Behavioral Therapy Practices:

Cognitive-behavioral therapy (CBT) has emerged as a prominent approach in the treatment of various psychological disorders, employing a structured and problem-focused methodology.

When considering the implications for CBT practices in the context of emotional conditioning theories, particularly differentiation and generalization, it becomes evident that these principles can significantly enrich the therapeutic process. By integrating Watsonian concepts into CBT, therapists can tailor interventions to address individualized emotional responses and broaden the scope of exposure techniques in therapy.

Incorporating differentiation into CBT involves a heightened awareness of the unique emotional triggers for each client. This necessitates thorough assessment and identification of specific stimuli that elicit primary and secondary emotional responses. Through systematic desensitization and gradual exposure to these triggers, CBT can introduce differentiated interventions that target distinct emotional reactions, thereby optimizing treatment outcomes. Furthermore, the incorporation of generalization principles in CBT allows for the transfer of learned responses from the therapy setting to real-world scenarios. Therapists can facilitate the generalization of adaptive coping mechanisms by promoting exposure exercises in various contexts, fostering the application of newly acquired skills beyond the treatment environment.

Integrating emotional conditioning principles with CBT enables the development of more tailored and effective intervention strategies for diverse clinical presentations. By recognizing the role of implicit learning and emotional associations, therapists can customize cognitive restructuring tasks to address conditioned emotional responses. This nuanced approach enhances the effectiveness of CBT in alleviating symptomatology and promoting lasting emotional regulation among clients.

Empirical evidence has also underscored the efficacy of combining differentiation and generalization principles within CBT protocols. Research studies have demonstrated the utility of integrating emotional conditioning techniques with CBT in the treatment of anxiety disorders, phobias, and post-traumatic stress disorder. These findings provide compelling support for the integration of Watsonian principles into contemporary CBT practices and highlight the potential for enhanced treatment outcomes when addressing complex emotional responses.

Given the multifaceted nature of emotional conditioning, it is imperative for practitioners to undergo specialized training to effectively implement these principles in CBT. Training programs that emphasize the integration of differentiation and generalization with established CBT modalities can equip therapists with the necessary skills to optimize therapeutic interventions. Additionally, ongoing supervision and mentorship are instrumental in refining the application of Watsonian theories within the dynamic landscape of CBT.

5. Integration with Modern Psychotherapeutic Methods:

By combining the principles of emotional differentiation and generalization with contemporary therapeutic approaches, clinicians can enhance the effectiveness of interventions across a wide range of psychological disorders. One crucial aspect of this integration involves the incorporation of cognitive-behavioral techniques, which have become fundamental in modern psychotherapy. Cognitive-behavioral therapy (CBT) emphasizes the interconnectedness between thoughts, emotions, and behaviors and aims to modify maladaptive patterns through targeted interventions. When integrated with Watson's theories, CBT gains additional depth and precision in understanding and addressing emotional responses. This synergy allows therapists to tailor interventions that specifically target the differentiation and generalization processes underlying emotional conditioning. Moreover, the incorporation of mindfulness-based strategies into therapeutic approaches further enriches the integration with Watsonian theory. Mindfulness practices encourage individuals to observe their thoughts and emotions without judgment, fostering greater awareness and acceptance of internal experiences. This aligns closely with the principles of emotional differentiation, promoting the discernment and articulation of distinct emotional states. Additionally, the integration of Watson's theories with trauma-focused interventions has shown promise in addressing the complex manifestations of post-traumatic stress disorder (PTSD) and related conditions. Techniques such as eye movement desensitization and reprocessing (EMDR) and narrative exposure therapy (NET) can be augmented by an understanding of differentiation and generalization processes, providing more nuanced and effective treatment for individuals with traumatic experiences. Exploring how Watsonian theory aligns with humanistic and experiential therapies also illuminates new avenues for integrative practice. Humanistic approaches emphasize empathy, authenticity, and the promotion of personal growth, while experiential therapies prioritize emotional exploration and processing in the therapeutic setting. By applying the concepts of differentiation and generalization within these frameworks, clinicians can deepen their understanding of clients' emotional responses and facilitate profound therapeutic change. It is vital for clinicians to receive comprehensive training in integrating Watsonian principles with modern psychotherapeutic methods to ensure ethical and competent practice. Supervision, continuing education, and adherence to professional guidelines are essential in managing this integration while upholding high standards of care.

6. Training and Implementation in Therapeutic Environments:

In order to effectively apply Watsonian principles in therapeutic environments, it is imperative to establish comprehensive training programs for mental health professionals. These programs should not only provide theoretical knowledge of emotional conditioning but also offer practical skills in behavioral interventions rooted in this framework. The training should encompass a multidisciplinary approach, drawing from psychology, psychiatry, and counseling to ensure a holistic understanding of client needs and effective implementation of techniques. Furthermore, ongoing professional development initiatives are essential to keep practitioners abreast of the latest research and advancements in the field. Once equipped with the requisite knowledge and skills, practitioners can then embark on the implementation phase. This involves creating a conducive therapeutic environment that fosters trust and collaboration between the therapist and the client. Practitioners need to adeptly apply differentiation and generalization techniques tailored to individual client needs. They must exhibit empathy and sensitivity while addressing the client's emotional responses and modifying maladaptive behaviors. Real-world simulations and supervised practice sessions can aid in refining application skills before engaging with actual clients. Integration with existing therapeutic modalities and initializing collaborative partnerships within multidisciplinary teams can enhance the efficacy of Watsonian-based interventions. Moving beyond theoretical understanding and practical implementation, ensuring ethical considerations in clinical application is paramount. Practitioners must uphold confidentiality, informed consent, and respect for autonomy throughout the therapeutic process. Professional supervision and regular peer consultations serve as mechanisms for maintaining ethical standards and continuous improvement in service delivery.

7. Ethical Considerations in Clinical Application:

As the utilization of Watsonian theories grows within clinical settings, it becomes imperative to thoroughly assess and address the ethical dimensions associated with their application. The fundamental principle guiding the ethical considerations in clinical applications of emotional conditioning is the well-being of the clients. This necessitates a delicate balance between the potential benefits of employing differentiation and generalization techniques and the possible risks or adverse effects. One primary ethical consideration revolves around informed consent and transparency in treatment approaches rooted in Watson's theories. Therapists must ensure that clients have a comprehensive understanding of the therapeutic processes, including how emotional differentiation and generalization techniques will be implemented, and the potential outcomes they may experience.

Additionally, ensuring confidentiality and privacy is paramount when incorporating these methods into clinical practice. Given the nature of emotional conditioning interventions, maintaining client privacy and protecting sensitive information becomes even more critical. Therapists must adhere to professional standards of confidentiality while integrating Watsonian principles into their therapeutic strategies.

The use of differentiated emotional responses and generalization techniques demands a keen awareness of potential power differentials between therapists and clients. Ethical practice requires therapists to continually monitor their interactions to prevent any misuse of influence and ensure that the client's autonomy and agency remain central to the therapeutic process. Moreover, therapists should regularly evaluate the impact of emotional conditioning interventions on the client's sense of control and self-determination.

Another ethical consideration involves the potential for unintended emotional distress or exacerbation of existing conditions. While differentiation and generalization techniques hold promise in treating various emotional disorders, therapists must diligently assess and minimize the risk of re-traumatization or overwhelming emotional responses. Efforts to create a safe and supportive environment during the implementation of these methods are essential.

Discussions surrounding the influence of societal and cultural factors on emotional conditioning interventions call for vigilant attention to diversity and inclusivity. Practitioners must recognize and respect the cultural nuances that shape emotional experiences and responses, ensuring that therapeutic applications align with the individual's cultural background and values.

CONTROVERSIES AND COUNTERARGUMENTS

Historical Disputes and Evolving Perspectives

The early years of emotional conditioning witnessed significant debate and contention among scholars and practitioners regarding the validity and ethical implications of the process. Critics of emotional conditioning argued that the initial research lacked rigor and failed to account for individual differences in response to conditioning stimuli. Moreover, historical disputes surfaced regarding the generalization of conditioned emotional responses across different contexts and stimuli. Some prominent psychologists challenged the reductionist approach of emotional conditioning, claiming that it oversimplified the complexity of human emotions and cognitive processes. As emotional conditioning theories evolved, disputes arose concerning the interpretation of empirical findings, leading to conflicting perspectives within the academic community. These disagreements contributed to the fragmentation of theories and approaches to emotional conditioning, highlighting the need for a comprehensive and nuanced understanding of the phenomenon. Over time, evolving perspectives incorporated interdisciplinary insights from cognitive psychology, neuroscience, and behavioral economics, prompting a reevaluation of historical disputes. Furthermore, historical disputes spurred rigorous methodological advancements, such as controlled experimental designs and longitudinal studies, aimed at addressing critics' concerns and bolstering the credibility of emotional conditioning research.

Criticism from Cognitive Psychology

Cognitive psychology offers a robust critique of emotional conditioning, asserting that the process of conditioning oversimplifies the complex interplay of cognitive processes, emotions, and behavior. Critics argue that emotional conditioning neglects the cognitive aspect involved in the formation and expression of emotions, emphasizing only the Pavlovian association of stimuli and responses. This narrow focus obscures the mental mechanisms that influence emotional experiences and reactions.

Cognitive psychologists contend that emotional conditioning fails to account for individual differences in cognitive functioning, such as attention, memory, and perception, which significantly shape emotional responses. They emphasize the role of cognitive appraisal in determining the subjective significance of stimuli and its impact on emotional states. This perspective challenges the deterministic nature of emotional conditioning, proposing that internal cognitive processes mediate between external stimuli and emotional outcomes.

Critics from cognitive psychology highlight the limitations of emotional conditioning in addressing complex human emotions, such as moral values, social judgments, and self-reflective emotions. They argue that these higher-order emotions involve sophisticated cognitive processes, reflective reasoning, and contextual understanding, which transcend the simplistic stimulus-response framework of emotional conditioning. By underscoring the inadequacy of emotional conditioning in capturing the richness and variability of human emotional experiences, cognitive psychology advocates for a more comprehensive approach that integrates cognitive factors into the study of emotions.

Additionally, cognitive psychology advances the notion that emotions are not merely predetermined by associative learning but are heavily influenced by individuals' cognitive interpretations, attributions, and beliefs about their experiences. This suggests that emotional conditioning overlooks the crucial role of cognition in shaping emotional meaning and regulation. Moreover, cognitive psychologists stress the significance of higher-level cognitive functions, such as language, problem-solving, and decision-making, in modulating emotional responses, which emotional conditioning fails to fully acknowledge.

Ethical Considerations and Misapplication Concerns

Ethical considerations surrounding emotional conditioning encompass a wide array of complex issues that have sparked debates among scholars, practitioners, and ethicists. One of the primary concerns revolves around the potential misuse or manipulation of individuals' emotions for purposes that may not align with their best interests. Researchers and practitioners must address the ethical implications of instigating emotional responses in individuals, especially in vulnerable populations such as children, individuals with mental health challenges, or those under duress. The question of informed consent and the limits of ethical experimentation in emotional conditioning research is a critical focal point. It necessitates thoughtful reflection and stringent adherence to ethical guidelines to ensure the protection of participants' autonomy and well-being. Furthermore, misapplication concerns often arise in the context of commercial or persuasive endeavors, where emotional conditioning techniques may be employed to influence consumer behavior or political decisions. This raises questions about the ethical boundaries of using emotional conditioning in marketing, advertising, or public opinion shaping, and prompts considerations regarding transparency, accountability, and the potential for exploitation. Additionally, the potential for unintended psychological harm from poorly executed or inadequately monitored emotional conditioning interventions cannot be overlooked. There is an inherent responsibility to mitigate any adverse effects and uphold the principle of nonmaleficence in the application of emotional conditioning. The nexus between ethics, power dynamics, and the influence of emotional conditioning underscores the need for a nuanced understanding of the ethical implications and the creation of robust safeguards.

Debates on Methodological Rigor

Critics have raised significant concerns about the validity and reliability of research methodologies employed in the investigation of emotional conditioning phenomena. One major point of contention revolves around the diverse approaches to experimental design and measurement, leading to ongoing disputes regarding the robustness of findings and the generalizability of conclusions.

A central aspect of this debate pertains to the selection of appropriate stimuli and experimental paradigms to elicit and assess emotional responses. Researchers argue that the clarity and consistency in defining emotional stimuli and the method of elicitation play a crucial role in ensuring the internal and external validity of findings. Conversely, opponents posit that the inherent subjectivity and variability in emotional experiences present formidable challenges to achieving methodological rigor in experimental designs. Furthermore, debates persist regarding the optimal utilization of control conditions and counterbalancing procedures to minimize confounds and enhance the reliability of observed emotional responses.

Another key contention revolves around the utility and limitations of traditional behavioral and self-report measures in capturing the intricacies of emotional conditioning processes. Proponents assert that these measures yield valuable insights into the cognitive and affective dimensions of emotional responses. However, skeptics argue that reliance on subjective self-reports and behavioral indicators may introduce bias and overlook nuanced aspects of emotional reactivity, emphasizing the need for more objective and ecologically valid assessment tools.

The ongoing discourse on methodological rigor encompasses critical evaluation of data analysis techniques and statistical procedures employed in emotional conditioning research. The appropriateness of statistical assumptions, the management of outliers, and the interpretation of effect sizes are among the focal points of contention, shaping the broader dialogue on the credibility and reproducibility of empirical findings in this domain.

Challenges in Replication and Verification

Replication and verification are essential cornerstones of scientific inquiry, including the field of emotional conditioning. However, researchers and scholars encounter numerous challenges in replicating and verifying experimental findings in this domain. One of the primary challenges lies in the inherent complexity of human emotions and behavior, which renders precise replication difficult. Emotions are dynamic and multifaceted, influenced by an array of internal and external variables that are often challenging to control across different experimental settings. Furthermore, the ethical considerations associated with inducing and manipulating emotions in controlled laboratory conditions present additional hurdles to exact replication.

Another significant obstacle is the variability in research methodologies employed across different studies. Variations in the design of experiments, such as the selection of stimuli, measurement techniques, and participant characteristics, contribute to inconsistencies in replication efforts. Additionally, the lack of standardized protocols and guidelines for conducting emotional conditioning studies further complicates the replication process. The absence of consensus on key methodological aspects hampers comparability between studies and diminishes the reliability of replicated results.

The inherent subjectivity of emotional experiences adds a layer of complexity to replication endeavors. Unlike physical phenomena that can be objectively measured and quantified, emotional responses are intrinsically subjective and may vary widely among individuals. This subjectivity introduces a degree of unpredictability into replication attempts, making it challenging to achieve consistent results across different populations and cultural contexts.

Further exacerbating these challenges is the publication bias within the academic community. Positive or statistically significant results are more likely to be published, leading to an incomplete representation of the true scope of findings. As a result, replication efforts may encounter difficulties in corroborating initially reported outcomes, especially if non-significant or negative results are less frequently disseminated.

To address these hurdles, concerted efforts towards promoting transparency, rigorous standardization of methodologies, and systematic documentation of replication attempts are imperative. Establishing comprehensive databases for storing both successful and unsuccessful replication studies can provide valuable insights into the factors influencing variability and the generalizability of emotional conditioning phenomena. Collaborative initiatives aimed at fostering open dialogue among researchers and facilitating data sharing can enhance the reliability and reproducibility of findings in the field, ultimately advancing our understanding of emotional conditioning.

Role of Biological Factors

While traditional behaviorist perspectives predominantly emphasize the influence of external stimuli and environmental factors on shaping emotional responses, there is a growing body of evidence that underscores the significant contribution of biological mechanisms in this complex process. Recent advances in neuroscience have unraveled the interplay between brain structures, neurotransmitters, and genetic predispositions in the formation and modulation of emotional reactions. Studies utilizing neuroimaging techniques, such as functional magnetic resonance imaging (fMRI) and positron emission tomography (PET), have revealed the activation patterns of key brain regions associated with emotional processing, including the amygdala, prefrontal cortex, and insular cortex. These findings provide compelling support for the argument that neural substrates play a crucial role in mediating emotional conditioning.

Research in the field of psychopharmacology has elucidated the impact of various neurotransmitter systems, such as serotonin and dopamine, on the encoding and extinction of conditioned emotional responses. Pharmacological interventions targeting these neurotransmitter pathways have demonstrated the potential to modulate emotional reactivity and mitigate maladaptive conditioning, thereby highlighting the involvement of biochemistry in shaping emotional behaviors.

Genetic investigations have shed light on the heritability of certain emotional traits and susceptibilities to conditioning processes. Variations in genes encoding for proteins involved in stress regulation, fear learning, and neural plasticity have been linked to individual differences in emotional responsiveness and vulnerability to developing anxiety-related disorders through conditioning paradigms.

Despite these compelling scientific revelations, it is evident that the integration of biological perspectives into the overarching framework of emotional conditioning remains relatively underemphasized in traditional behavioral theories. This oversight limits our comprehensive understanding of the multifaceted nature of emotional learning and adaptation, hindering the development of more holistic and efficacious therapeutic strategies.

It is imperative for contemporary researchers and practitioners in the field of psychology to acknowledge and integrate the nuanced influence of biological factors in emotional conditioning paradigms. By adopting an interdisciplinary approach that synthesizes insights from neuroscience, genetics, and psychopharmacology with established behavioral theories, we can pave the way for a more nuanced, sophisticated comprehension of emotional conditioning processes. This integrated perspective holds promise for refining existing therapeutic interventions and fostering the emergence of novel treatment modalities that account for the interplay between psychological, environmental, and biological determinants of emotional behavior.

Interdisciplinary Critiques

Advancements in neuroscience have stimulated profound discussions and critiques regarding the role of biological factors in emotional conditioning. In recent years, interdisciplinary research initiatives have shed light on the interplay between neural mechanisms and emotional responses, challenging traditional perspectives within the sphere of behavioral psychology. Neuroscientific investigations have unraveled the neurobiological underpinnings of emotional conditioning, elucidating how synaptic plasticity, neurotransmitter systems, and neural circuitry contribute to the formation and modulation of conditioned emotional responses. Such insights have sparked debates about the extent to which cognitive and affective processes are inherently intertwined with underlying neurobiological substrates.

Critics from the neuroscientific community advocate for a holistic approach that integrates knowledge from behavioral psychology with findings from neurobiology. They argue that exclusive emphasis on external stimuli and observable behaviors neglects the crucial contributions of neurobiological elements in shaping emotional responses. Additionally, neuroscientific evidence has raised questions about the generalizability of classical emotional conditioning paradigms across diverse populations, emphasizing the need to consider individual differences in neural architecture and function. Furthermore, the emerging field of affective neuroscience has emphasized the dynamic nature of emotional states, highlighting the relevance of temporal dynamics and contextual factors that influence emotional learning and memory processes.

Insights from functional neuroimaging techniques, such as fMRI and EEG, have provided compelling evidence regarding the neural substrates involved in the extinction and reconsolidation of conditioned emotional responses. These findings have ramifications for therapeutic interventions, as they underscore the potential of targeting specific neural circuits to modulate maladaptive emotional reactions.

FUTURE DIRECTIONS IN EMOTIONAL CONDITIONING

Emerging Theoretical Frameworks

Advancements in the field of emotional conditioning have prompted an exploration of emerging theoretical frameworks that expand our understanding and application of this fundamental concept in psychology. In recent years, researchers and scholars have delved into novel theoretical models that go beyond traditional stimulus-response paradigms, offering comprehensive perspectives on the complexities of emotional conditioning.

One significant area of focus revolves around the integration of cognitive processes within emotional conditioning models. This amalgamation aims to elucidate the interplay between cognitive appraisals, belief systems, and emotional responses, thereby providing a more nuanced comprehension of how conditioned emotions manifest and evolve over time. By articulating the ways in which cognitive factors influence the acquisition and expression of conditioned emotions, these innovative frameworks enhance our grasp of the underlying mechanisms governing emotional conditioning.

Contemporary theoretical advancements emphasize the dynamic nature of emotional conditioning, moving beyond static associations between stimuli and emotional responses. The recognition of contextual factors, temporal dynamics, and individual differences has paved the way for more holistic models that capture the intricacies of emotional conditioning processes. From examining the role of situational cues in eliciting conditioned emotional reactions to elucidating the impact of developmental stages on the formation of emotional associations, these progressive frameworks afford a comprehensive view of emotional conditioning that transcends traditional, linear paradigms.

Emerging theoretical models delve into the interconnection between emotional conditioning and social learning theories, shedding light on how interpersonal interactions and societal contexts shape the development and perpetuation of conditioned emotional responses. This integration underscores the importance of sociocultural factors in modulating emotional conditioning processes, encapsulating the complex interweaving of individual experiences within broader social and cultural milieus.

Technological Innovations in Research Methodologies

In recent years, the integration of innovative technologies has revolutionized data collection, analysis, and interpretation, leading to a deeper understanding of emotional processes and their conditioning. One of the most notable technological innovations is the utilization of neuroimaging techniques such as functional magnetic resonance imaging (fMRI) and electroencephalography (EEG) to elucidate the neural mechanisms underlying emotional responses. These non-invasive and high-resolution imaging methods provide researchers with unprecedented insights into the neural circuits involved in emotional conditioning, facilitating the identification of specific brain regions implicated in various emotional states.

The advent of virtual reality (VR) has opened new avenues for studying emotional responses in controlled and immersive environments. By simulating diverse scenarios and stimuli, researchers can systematically investigate the impact of different stimuli on emotional learning and subsequent conditioned responses. The use of VR not only enhances the ecological validity of experimental paradigms but also offers opportunities to develop targeted interventions for individuals with maladaptive emotional responses.

Additionally, the integration of machine learning algorithms and big data analytics has empowered researchers to discern complex patterns within extensive datasets derived from emotional conditioning studies. Through the application of predictive modeling and pattern recognition techniques, researchers can identify subtle nuances in emotional reactivity and predict individual differences in the acquisition and extinction of conditioned emotional responses. This data-driven approach not only accelerates the pace of discovery but also lays the groundwork for personalized interventions tailored to individuals' unique emotional profiles.

Advancements in psychophysiological monitoring devices, such as wearable biosensors and mobile applications, have enabled real-time assessment of emotional states in naturalistic settings. The continuous monitoring of physiological markers, including heart rate variability, electrodermal activity, and facial expressions, provides a comprehensive understanding of emotional responses in everyday life, transcending the limitations of lab-based experiments.

Interdisciplinary Approaches and Collaborative Efforts

As the field of emotional conditioning continues to evolve, there has been a growing recognition of the need for interdisciplinary approaches and collaborative efforts to advance our understanding of emotional responses and their conditioning. Interdisciplinary collaboration brings together experts from diverse fields such as psychology, neuroscience, psychiatry, artificial intelligence, and sociology, among others. By integrating knowledge and methodologies from these distinct disciplines, researchers can gain a more comprehensive understanding of emotional conditioning, encompassing its psychological, biological, social, and technological dimensions. This holistic approach not only enriches the depth of investigation but also fosters innovation and creativity by bridging different perspectives.

One illustrative example of interdisciplinary collaboration is the fusion of neuroscience and computational modeling to elucidate the neural mechanisms underlying emotional conditioning. Through collaborations between neuroscientists and computer scientists, sophisticated computational models are being developed to simulate and analyze complex neural networks involved in emotional learning and memory. This integration of expertise allows for a deeper exploration of the neural circuitry implicated in emotional responses and opens new avenues for intervention strategies.

Interdisciplinary approaches extend beyond the scope of academia and research, embracing partnerships with industry and technology sectors. Collaborations with technology companies and software developers have led to the creation of innovative tools for assessing and modulating emotional states, thereby enhancing the potential applications of emotional conditioning in mental health interventions and well-being enhancement programs.

In addition to interdisciplinary research initiatives, collaborative efforts involving clinicians, therapists, and educators are paramount in translating theoretical advancements into practical and effective interventions. By fostering alliances between researchers and practitioners, insights derived from cutting-edge research can be directly translated into evidence-based therapies and educational frameworks. This synergy not only accelerates the implementation of novel conditioning techniques but also ensures that they are tailored to address real-world challenges and diverse clinical populations.

Genetic and Neuroscientific Insights

Genetic studies have identified specific genes associated with emotional regulation, fear response, and susceptibility to conditioning, offering valuable insights into individual differences and predispositions. Furthermore, neuroimaging techniques such as functional magnetic resonance imaging (fMRI) and positron emission tomography (PET) have allowed researchers to visualize the neural mechanisms underlying emotional conditioning, elucidating the neural circuits involved in the acquisition, consolidation, and extinction of conditioned responses.

The identification of candidate genes implicated in emotional processing has opened new avenues for investigating the heritability of emotional traits and vulnerability to maladaptive conditioning. Genome-wide association studies and gene expression profiling have uncovered potential genetic markers linked to heightened emotional reactivity or resilience, providing a foundation for personalized approaches to emotional conditioning interventions. Moreover, epigenetic modifications, influenced by environmental factors, contribute to the dynamic regulation of gene expression in response to conditioning experiences, offering a nuanced perspective on the interaction between nature and nurture in shaping emotional responses.

In parallel, neuroscientific investigations have delineated the key brain regions and neurotransmitter systems involved in emotional learning and memory. The amygdala, prefrontal cortex, hippocampus, and insula have emerged as central nodes in the neural network orchestrating conditioned emotional responses, while neurochemical signaling pathways, including those mediated by dopamine, serotonin, and glutamate, modulate the strength and persistence of conditioned associations. Understanding the neural substrates of emotional conditioning not only enhances our comprehension of psychiatric conditions characterized by aberrant emotional processing but also informs the development of targeted pharmacological interventions and neuromodulation techniques to alleviate pathological conditioning.

Integration of genetic and neuroscientific findings holds immense promise for the future of emotional conditioning research and application. By elucidating the biological underpinnings of individual variation in emotional reactivity and susceptibility to conditioning, this interdisciplinary approach paves the way for precision medicine in the field of mental health. Harnessing genetic and neural insights can guide the refinement of therapeutic strategies, ranging from tailored exposure therapies to novel pharmacogenomic interventions, aimed at optimizing clinical outcomes and fostering emotional resilience. However, ethical considerations surrounding the use of genetic information and neural interventions necessitate careful deliberation and responsible implementation to ensure the ethical and equitable application of these advancements in the context of emotional conditioning.

Applications in Digital Mental Health Interventions

The integration of digital technologies into mental health interventions represents a significant advancement in the field of emotional conditioning. Digital mental health interventions encompass various technological tools and platforms, including but not limited to mobile applications, virtual reality simulations, wearable devices, and online therapy programs. These innovative solutions offer unprecedented opportunities to personalize and optimize emotional conditioning techniques for individuals across diverse demographics and geographical locations.

One of the key advantages of digital mental health interventions is their ability to enhance accessibility to evidence-based emotional conditioning programs. Individuals can now access therapeutic resources and interventions remotely, circumventing traditional barriers such as geographical distance, transportation limitations, and stigmas associated with seeking in-person therapy. This democratization of mental health services has the potential to reach individuals who may have otherwise been unable or hesitant to seek help, thereby expanding the scope and impact of emotional conditioning therapies.

Digital platforms provide unique capabilities for real-time monitoring and data collection, enabling practitioners to gain insights into the effectiveness of emotional conditioning strategies. By leveraging data analytics and machine learning algorithms, these interventions can adapt and evolve based on individual responses, fostering a dynamic and personalized approach to emotional wellness. Additionally, the integration of biofeedback mechanisms through wearable devices allows for the continuous assessment of emotional states, facilitating targeted interventions and timely support.

In the sphere of digital mental health, virtual reality simulations hold tremendous promise for immersive exposure therapy, a cornerstone of emotional conditioning in addressing phobias and anxiety disorders. Through sophisticated virtual environments, individuals can safely confront and habituate to triggering stimuli, accelerating the process of emotional desensitization and relearning. Moreover, virtual reality platforms offer a controlled and customizable setting for therapists to tailor emotional conditioning scenarios, catering to the specific needs and sensitivities of each individual.

As with any emerging domain, ethical considerations are paramount in the development and deployment of digital mental health interventions. Ensuring data privacy, informed consent, and the responsible use of artificial intelligence algorithms are critical aspects that require ongoing attention and regulation. Moreover, the integration of cultural competence and inclusivity in the design of digital interventions is essential to address diverse perspectives and ensure equitable access.

The advent of digital mental health interventions heralds a new era in the application of emotional conditioning, presenting an array of opportunities to refine and expand the reach of therapeutic practices. By harnessing the potential of technology in conjunction with evidence-based emotional conditioning principles, the field stands poised to transform the landscape of mental health care, empowering individuals to cultivate resilience, emotional well-being, and transformative personal growth.

Personalization of Conditioning Techniques for Enhanced Therapies

Tailoring emotional conditioning processes to individual characteristics, preferences, and life experiences can significantly augment the efficacy and sustainability of behavioral therapies. By recognizing the unique cognitive and emotional profiles of each client, practitioners can design interventions that resonate more deeply with their specific needs and circumstances. This personalized approach fosters a stronger sense of empowerment and agency, thereby promoting greater engagement and commitment to the therapeutic process.

Personalization of conditioning techniques involves a comprehensive assessment of various factors, including but not limited to personality traits, cultural background, trauma history, and coping mechanisms. Integrating this information allows for the formulation of targeted intervention strategies that address the nuanced complexities of an individual's emotional and behavioral responses. Furthermore, the utilization of advanced assessment tools, such as neuroimaging techniques and psychophysiological measurements, enables a deeper understanding of an individual's neural correlates and autonomic regulatory patterns, thus informing the customization of conditioning protocols.

In contemporary practice, the integration of digital technologies has notably transformed the landscape of personalized conditioning techniques. Digital platforms and applications provide avenues for continuous monitoring and data collection, allowing for real-time adjustments and refinements to conditioning protocols based on ongoing feedback and progress tracking. Moreover, virtual reality (VR) and augmented reality (AR) technologies have emerged as promising tools for creating immersive and personalized environments conducive to emotional exposure and desensitization, especially in the context of anxiety disorders and phobias.

Ethical considerations accompany the implementation of personalized conditioning techniques, emphasizing the importance of informed consent, confidentiality, and respect for autonomy. Practitioners must manage the ethical dilemmas surrounding the collection and utilization of sensitive personal data, ensuring the protection of individuals' privacy and dignity throughout the customization process. Additionally, ongoing ethical discourse is essential to address the potential implications of using personalized interventions, particularly in addressing power differentials and cultural sensitivities within the therapeutic relationship.

Ethical Considerations in Future Research and Practices

The future of emotional conditioning research and application necessitates a steadfast commitment to ethical considerations that uphold the rights, well-being, and autonomy of individuals participating in studies or undergoing therapeutic interventions. As advancements in technologies and methodologies continue to unfold, researchers and practitioners face the imperative responsibility of ensuring ethical guidelines are not only upheld but also enriched in response to evolving scientific landscapes. Fundamental ethical considerations encompass the informed consent process, confidentiality and privacy safeguards, and the mitigation of potential risks or harms to participants. With the integration of advanced neuroscientific and genetic insights into emotional conditioning, ethical scrutiny must be heightened to address concerns related to potential stigmatization, misinformation, and the responsible use of sensitive information. Moreover, as personalized conditioning techniques gain traction for tailored therapies, the ethical implications of individualized interventions call for a critical discourse on the balance between efficacy and the protection of personal boundaries and beliefs. Beyond the confines of research laboratories, the global dissemination of emotional conditioning practices prompts an exploration of cross-cultural ethics. Respect for cultural diversity, contextual sensitivity, and equitable access to beneficial interventions constitute pivotal ethical considerations in fostering a harmonious intersection between diverse belief systems and scientific progress. As the field of emotional conditioning strives for global impact, recognizing and reconciling ethical imperatives across different societal norms and values becomes an essential pursuit. In addition to proactive ethical anticipations, integrating a reflective and responsive approach is crucial. This entails the continual reassessment of ethical frameworks in tandem with technological, social, and political dynamics. Embracing transparency and accountability in decision-making processes not only safeguards ethical integrity but also reinforces public trust and confidence in the responsible advancement of emotional conditioning research and applications. Ultimately, ethical considerations in future emotional conditioning endeavors are foundational pillars that uphold the moral compass guiding the trajectory of research, clinical practice, and societal implementation.

Global Perspectives and Cross-Cultural Studies

The exploration of global perspectives and cross-cultural studies in the context of emotional conditioning broadens our understanding of how psychological phenomena operate across diverse societies and cultural backgrounds. These endeavors acknowledge the influence of cultural, societal, and environmental factors on emotional responses and conditioning processes, paving the way for a more comprehensive and inclusive approach to research and application. By delving into the examination of emotional conditioning in various cultural contexts, researchers can elucidate the similarities and differences in the mechanisms, triggers, and manifestations of conditioned emotional responses. Consequently, this not only enhances our theoretical frameworks but also contributes to the development of tailored interventions that accommodate cultural nuances and sensitivities. Furthermore, cross-cultural studies enable the identification of universal principles of emotional conditioning as well as culture-specific variations, shedding light on the interplay between nature and nurture in shaping emotional experiences. Through collaborative efforts with experts from diverse cultural backgrounds, researchers can leverage their collective knowledge and insights to establish culturally sensitive guidelines and best practices for emotional conditioning research and therapeutic applications. Moreover, global perspectives also facilitate the dissemination of knowledge and evidence-based practices across borders, enriching the global mental health landscape with culturally informed approaches that resonate with different populations. The ethical considerations inherent in conducting cross-cultural studies emphasize the importance of respecting cultural norms, values, and traditions, thereby fostering trust and rapport within communities. It is imperative to recognize the potential impact of emotional conditioning research on societal beliefs, norms, and practices, and to ensure that such investigations align with ethical guidelines and promote cultural competence. As such, the integration of global perspectives and cross-cultural studies in the sphere of emotional conditioning not only amplifies the richness of empirical data but also reinforces the ethical responsibility to uphold the dignity and diversity of individuals and communities worldwide.

Policy Implications and Societal Impact

As our understanding of emotional conditioning continues to evolve, it becomes crucial for policymakers to consider the potential impact of this knowledge on the development of interventions and support systems. In the arena of mental health policy, insights from emotional conditioning research can inform the design of targeted interventions for individuals struggling with anxiety, phobias, and trauma-related disorders. By integrating evidence-based emotional conditioning techniques into therapeutic frameworks, policymakers can contribute to the enhancement of mental health services, thereby promoting resilience and recovery among affected populations. Furthermore, within the educational landscape, recognizing the impact of emotional conditioning on learning and behavior can guide the establishment of supportive environments within schools. Policies geared towards fostering emotional intelligence, empathy, and positive peer interactions can be informed by research findings in emotional conditioning, ultimately contributing to the holistic development of students. Moreover, the societal impact of emotional conditioning research extends beyond individual well-being and education. It intersects with broader social issues such as public health initiatives, community resilience, and workplace dynamics. By acknowledging the influence of emotional responses on decision-making processes, policymakers can incorporate strategies derived from emotional conditioning principles to address societal challenges related to risk perception, health behaviors, and conflict resolution. Additionally, the integration of emotional conditioning insights into workplace policies and organizational practices can lead to the cultivation of healthier and more supportive work environments, ultimately impacting productivity, job satisfaction, and employee well-being.

Conclusions and Vision for Progressive Development

The exploration of policy implications and societal impact highlights the integral role of emotional conditioning in shaping not only individual well-being but also broader social dynamics. As we conclude this comprehensive study on emotional conditioning, it is essential to articulate a vision for progressive development in the field, encompassing both research and practical applications. Looking ahead, it is imperative to foster greater collaboration between policymakers, researchers, and practitioners to ensure that the insights gained from this domain are effectively integrated into mental health policies and interventions.

One key emphasis for progressive development involves the need for evidence-based guidelines and standards that govern the ethical implementation of emotional conditioning techniques in therapeutic settings. Such guidelines should prioritize the well-being and autonomy of individuals, promoting informed consent, transparency, and ongoing evaluation of the efficacy and potential risks associated with these interventions. Additionally, continuous dialogue and engagement with diverse stakeholders, including ethicists, clinicians, and advocacy groups, are pivotal in identifying and addressing emerging ethical considerations.

In envisioning the future trajectory of emotional conditioning, there is a pressing need to harness technological advancements such as artificial intelligence, virtual reality, and mobile applications to enhance the accessibility and effectiveness of conditioning-based interventions. These innovations have the potential to revolutionize personalized therapies, enabling tailored approaches that consider an individual's unique psychological profile, life experiences, and cultural background. Consequently, interdisciplinary collaborations with experts in computer science, data analytics, and human-computer interaction will be instrumental in driving these developments forward.

In line with the spirit of continuous improvement, fostering a vibrant research ecosystem dedicated to unraveling the neurobiological underpinnings of emotional conditioning is vital for advancing the field. Integrating genetic and neuroscientific insights offers promising avenues for refining our understanding of individual differences in emotional reactivity and resilience. Furthermore, the synthesis of knowledge across disciplines, including psychology, psychiatry, and neuroscience, can precipitate paradigm-shifting discoveries that may inform the next generation of targeted interventions and treatment protocols.

As we embark on this journey of progress and transformation, it is essential to underscore the significance of cultivating a global perspective. Cross-cultural studies and collaborative initiatives with international counterparts are pivotal in elucidating the universality and context-specific nature of emotional conditioning phenomena. By embracing diversity and cross-pollination of ideas, the field stands to benefit from a rich tapestry of insights, thereby enriching the repertoire of evidence-based practices and culturally sensitive interventions.

Finally, the overarching vision for progressive development in emotional conditioning must prioritize fostering resilience, empathy, and emotional well-being on a societal scale. This entails engaging with education systems, community organizations, and policymakers to integrate knowledge about emotional conditioning into public health initiatives, educational curricula, and mental health awareness campaigns. By nurturing emotionally intelligent and resilient societies, we pave the way for a future where individuals are empowered to regulate their inner landscapes with insight and compassion.

WATSON'S 20 QUOTES ON EMOTIONAL CONDITIONING

On the Fundamentals of Emotional Conditioning

"The behaviorist believes that all behavior, including emotional responses, is learned through conditioning."

"We are able to take a neutral stimulus and, by pairing it with an unconditioned emotional stimulus, make it call out the emotional response originally given by the unconditioned stimulus."

"Fear can be experimentally produced in a child by suddenly striking a steel bar behind his head."

"The infant starts with a few simple emotional reactions—fear, rage, and love—and from these, through conditioning, the complex emotional life of the adult develops."

"The emotional responses of humans are not innate but are learned through environmental stimuli."

On Fear and Anxiety

"Fear can be observed by the following reaction with infants: crying, rapid breathing, eyes closing, or sudden jumping."

"Fear is evoked by only two stimuli that are unconditioned—a sudden noise or the loss of (physical) support."

"Fear can be conditioned in infants by pairing a neutral stimulus with an unconditioned stimulus."

"Fear can be generalized to other stimuli that resemble the original conditioned stimulus."

"Fear responses can persist over time and may not be easily extinguished."

On Rage and Aggression

“Rage is an innate response to the body movement of the child being constrained.”

“Rage can be conditioned in infants by restricting their movement.”

“Rage responses can be generalized to situations where the child feels restrained or controlled.”

“Rage can be observed by the following reaction with infants: screaming, stiffening of the body, and kicking.”

“Rage responses can persist over time and may be triggered by similar situations.”

On Love and Affection

“Love is an automatic response from infants when tickled, patted, or stroked lightly.”

“Love can be conditioned in infants by pairing a neutral stimulus with positive reinforcement.”

“Love responses can be generalized to other stimuli that resemble the original conditioned stimulus.”

“Love responses can persist over time and may not be easily extinguished.”

“Love is a learned behavior, not an innate emotion.”

www.ingramcontent.com/pod-product-compliance
Lightning Source LLC
LaVergne TN
LVHW052320200926
848481LV00002B/615
9798231792481